PLAYING
WITH
PURPOSE

PLAYING
WITH
PURPOSE

INSIDE THE LIVES AND FAITH OF
TOP NBA STARS—
KEVIN DURANT, KYLE KORVER, JEREMY LIN, AND MORE!

MIKE YORKEY

BARBOUR
PUBLISHING

Cover images (left to right): AP Photo/Tony Gutierrez; Rocky Widner/Getty; AP Photo/Lori Shepler

The author is represented by WordServe Literary Group, Ltd., Greg Johnson, Literary Agent, 10152 S. Knoll Circle, Highlands Ranch, CO 80130

Published by Barbour Publishing, Inc., P.O. Box 719, Uhrichsville, Ohio 44683 www.barbourbooks.com

Our mission is to publish and distribute inspirational products offering exceptional value and biblical encouragement to the masses.

 Member of the
Evangelical Christian
Publishers Association

Printed in the United States of America.

To NBA chaplains like Jeff Ryan of the Orlando Magic—
you're the unsung heroes.

CONTENTS

FOREWORD

BY ERNIE JOHNSON, HOST OF TNT'S *INSIDE THE NBA*

Back during the 1990s, the New York Knicks and Indiana Pacers were perennial playoff teams that developed quite a rivalry. Who can forget the feud between Pacers guard Reggie Miller and Knicks fan Spike Lee, who, from his courtside seat, gave Miller the business and then some?

The two teams grew to really dislike each other, and our TNT analysts, Charles Barkley and Kenny Smith, certainly had enough to talk about whenever the Knicks and Pacers squared off in the playoffs. With no love lost between two teams fighting over the same bone, their playoff series made for great television.

One time, either in 1999 or 2000, the Knicks and the Pacers were battling it out in the Eastern Conference finals. There was a day off between games, and the Knicks were staying in the same hotel as the TNT crew. I ran into Knicks guard Allan Houston in the lobby, and we were talking about some of the crazy things happening on the court when he casually mentioned, "A few of us are going to get together and have a little Bible study and get into the Word."

"Wow," I said. "Can I get in there, too?"

You see, a couple of years before, I had realized something major was missing in my life—a relationship with Jesus Christ. For forty-one years, my life had been all about me. Everything was in place: I had a great wife, Cheryl, four happy kids who gave me great joy, and a TV career in full ascendancy. I was living a performance-driven life as studio host for TNT Sports, quarterbacking coverage of the NBA, NFL, and Wimbledon tennis. My identity was tied up in what I did. You might as well have stamped a red TNT logo on my forehead—or "E.J."

But since everything was always about me, I was growing weary.

At a critical time in my life, a good friend came alongside me and explained that everything *doesn't* revolve around my existence—that there was more to life. He talked about God having a plan for me and how much He loves me. I had never really explored a personal relationship with Jesus Christ, so this was a revolutionary idea for me. I mean, I always knew God was there, and I knew Jesus Christ was there—but I had never put the two together.

When I heard that Jesus was holding out His hand, saying, "Come to me, all you who are weary and burdened, and I will give you rest," I grasped that hand. Oh, how I needed rest. Oh, how I needed that peace.

So when Allan Houston mentioned a Bible study during that off day, I invited myself in a New York minute.

Allan smiled and answered, "Sure, you can join us."

A couple of hours later, Allan, two or three other Knicks

players, and a couple of people from the New York front office got together in one of the team's meeting rooms. We circled up the chairs and dove into God's Word, and we had an awesome time.

Impromptu Bible studies like that built my faith, and I certainly needed that spiritual foundation when I faced a personal crisis a few years later. In 2003, I was diagnosed with non-Hodgkin's lymphoma, a low-grade and treatable cancer. My oncologist recommended that we "watch and wait," meaning we would monitor my condition with check-ups every four months with the option to begin treatment if and when I began showing symptoms of the illness.

Then, in late 2005, a lymph node near my left ear began swelling. That became noticeable to TNT viewers and prompted questions about my health. Now it was time to take more aggressive treatment measures. Beginning in June 2006, I skipped my usual summer responsibilities and submitted to six chemotherapy treatments. In my official press release, I noted that my family and I "continue, as we always have, in both good times and bad, to place our faith in Jesus Christ, and to trust God . . . period."

One of the good things about the chemotherapy treatments, besides the fact that they saved my life, was that I became just as bald as Sir Charles and Kenny the Jet. Then the cancer went into remission and my hair and eyebrows grew back.

When people ask me, "How did you get through that?" I repeat what I said in my press release: "Trust God . . . period," not "Trust God if this next test comes back the way I want it to . . . period."

I'm thanking God I'm still here. The 2011–12 NBA season will be my twenty-second on TNT. People often ask me how the professional game has changed over the years, and I like to quip that there are still five guys to a side and whoever scores the most points still wins. The game of basketball still captivates, still stirs our passions.

We have some wonderful Christian players, coaches, and front-office people in the NBA today, and you're going to read about some of them in this book. I think it takes a special guy to make a decision for Christ and continue to live for Him as an NBA player. That's because these professional athletes face so many temptations. Most professional basketball players are in their twenties, and the best advice I can give them—based on my long experience with life and the NBA—is to ask themselves, *How did I get here?*

I would advise them to look at the talents they have and ask these questions: Where did your talents come from? Who gave you the opportunity to develop them? Who gave you the ability to jump up and touch the top of the backboard? Were special people put into your life at just the right time to mold you, shape you, and lift your game to the NBA level?

Those kinds of questions are important no matter who you are or what you do. Who gave you your business acumen? Who gave you the ability to communicate? Who gave you the ability to lead others? And who gave you the ability to complete a variety of different tasks on time and on budget?

I understand that it's God who has given me the talent to broadcast live sporting events and host studio shows that require me to think on my feet, provide thoughtful analysis, ask interesting questions, and move in and out of commercials. And it's always live TV, where slip-ups aren't tolerated.

I know who gave me the talent to do what I do—the Lord. I've seen time and time again how He uses me in ways I never thought possible. One example took place during the 2007 NBA All-Star weekend in Las Vegas, Nevada. It was just a few months after I returned to the air following my chemotherapy treatments, and I was asked to emcee an Athletes in Action All-Star breakfast. The organizers asked me to deliver a speech, and I woke up the morning of the breakfast really wrestling with what I should say. I mapped my talk with a few notes in my hotel room, but as the start of the program neared, I still wasn't sure what I would share with those in attendance.

After I was introduced, I welcomed the guests and thanked them for making time that morning to be with us for such a worthy cause. But in the back of my mind, I was thinking, *Where am I going to go now?* When I opened my mouth, though, God gave me the right words to say.

"Has your life been touched by cancer?" I began. "Has your family's life been touched by cancer? You have a Friend. This is my cancer story."

I've heard from hundreds of people that my eight-minute talk was powerful and from the heart. (You can watch it on YouTube by typing in "Ernie Johnson cancer.") It was like God put His hand on my shoulder and said, "Stick with me, kid. I'll get you through this."

God, through His Son, Jesus Christ, is the one who created us and gave each of us unique gifts that make us part of the body of believers. If you keep that in mind, it keeps you centered and balanced. It keeps you from thinking about what a great guy or great gal you are. Instead, it keeps you—and me—focused on God and leaves you with this thought: *Wow, what a great God I have who has given me all these talents.*

The players and other people you are going to read about know exactly where their talent came from, which is why they are "playing with purpose."

INTRODUCTION

IT'S NOT AN EASY GIG,
PLAYING IN THE NBA

The year was 1993, and I (Mike Yorkey) was in my seventh year as editor of *Focus on the Family* magazine, the monthly periodical published by the Christian ministry founded by Dr. James Dobson.

The early '90s were great years to be the editor of a national magazine with a circulation in the millions. Something called the "Internet" was still the province of nerds on college campuses, so the terms *e-mail*, *websites*, *Google search*, and especially *LOL* were still unknown in the culture. When two-and-a–half-million copies of *Focus on the Family* magazine landed in people's homes every month, they got read—as long as that month's issue included compelling stories, helpful how-to articles, and emotional heart-tuggers.

In early 1993, I had a brainstorm for what I thought was a great idea: feature three young men in their twenties who were "willing to wait"—wait until marriage to have sex, that is. I wanted to explore how these guys were able to hold themselves back from the super-strong urge to get physical in a permissive society where the barriers to premarital sex were practically non-existent. Why were they *not* doing it when probably everyone they knew *was*? What safeguards did they equip themselves with to prevent their motors from overheating?

I discussed my idea with the editorial team, and I received nothing but thumbs up. Now came the hard part: finding three good-looking, cool, hip men in their twenties willing to tell five million readers they were virgins. And I wanted to give the story some added cachet, so I decided one of the three had to be a celebrity, someone in the public eye.

At Focus on the Family, we generally worked on our articles two to three months in advance of the magazine's release. This planning session took place toward the end of February, which meant our story wouldn't be published until June at the earliest.

June . . . that's baseball season. *Our celebrity could be a baseball player*, I thought. I figured there had to be someone in Major League Baseball who followed God's Word regarding premarital sexual behavior. And with twenty-eight major-league teams (this was before the Tampa Bay Rays and Arizona Diamondbacks joined the game) each sporting a twenty-five-man roster, I had a pool of seven hundred players to contact. I figured that if even half were married, there had to be at least one virgin among the never-married players who'd be willing to make a public stand.

I worked my Rolodex—yes, we still had those desktop rotary card indexes in those pre-smartphone days—and started dialing my contacts. After a week of putting out feelers, I came up with zilch. "Forget it," said one contact. "There are no virgins in Major League Baseball."

Maybe, maybe not, I thought. But as each lead proved fruitless, I had a sinking feeling I wouldn't find that special person I was looking for.

One day, I discussed my problem with Gary Lydic, a colleague at Focus on the Family. I explained who I was looking for—a Christian athlete who'd be willing to tell the world he was willing to wait. The sport didn't matter.

Among his other duties, Gary ran the annual Focus on the Family summer basketball camps. I had played in early morning pickup games with Gary and Dr. Dobson—more on that later—back when the ministry was headquartered in Arcadia, California. Gary was crazy about basketball as well as a great shooter with a velvet touch. I was sure he'd have some ideas for me.

Gary asked me if he could think about it, and the next day he called. "A.C. Green is your guy," he said. "He's the one you want to speak to."

I knew who A.C. Green was. I had grown up in Southern California and been a lifelong Lakers fan, starting with the Jerry West and Elgin Baylor days to the championship teams of Wilt Chamberlain and Magic Johnson. A.C. Green, who played on three Lakers championship teams, was one of those solid players every team needs—not a superstar but a star performer who plays defense and sweeps the boards. He was a power forward who played both ends of the court.

"How do I get hold of him?" I asked Gary.

"Call the Lakers and ask for the media relations department," he said. That meant dialing 411 for information, then calling the Lakers. I figured that if I got to talk to a live voice,

I'd probably get shuffled around.

I was looking at the local newspaper over lunchtime when I noticed that the Lakers would be in Denver the *very next night* to play the Nuggets. I was in luck, since the Lakers came to Denver only twice a year. Colorado Springs, by then the home of Focus on the Family headquarters, was only seventy miles south of Denver, a straight shot north on Interstate 25.

When I called the Nuggets front office, I was immediately put through to the media relations department. I explained who I was and why I was requesting a press pass, which would allow me access to the Lakers locker room after the game. "No problem, sir," said the young man helping me. "Your media pass will be waiting for you at Will Call."

I couldn't remember who won this unremarkable mid-season game between two sub-.500 teams, but thanks to the Internet, I found out that the Nuggets had beaten the Lakers 127–115 on March 2, 1993.

When the Lakers locker room was opened to the media after the game, just one reporter and I walked into a tomb-like space. The locker room was quiet because the Lakers had lost but also because Magic Johnson was gone. I still remember where I was on November 7, 1991—riding in my car in downtown Colorado Springs—when I heard the announcement over the radio that Magic had been diagnosed HIV-positive and was retiring from pro basketball. He was the first sports superstar to announce that he was HIV-positive, and that created quite a stir and remained a big story throughout the early 1990s. Magic said that he had contracted the virus as a result of having multiple sex partners over the years, adding that he didn't know from whom he contracted the virus or how long he had been infected.

As I moved about the locker room, I saw the Lakers' biggest star, James Worthy, lying buck naked on a trainer's table, getting rubbed down, while players like Vlade Divac and Byron Scott filtered in and out of the shower. We were still a few years away from the Kobe and Shaq era.

I approached my quarry, A.C. Green, as he was toweling off after his postgame shower. After introducing myself and holding up a recent copy of *Focus on the Family* magazine, I held up a mini-cassette recorder—A.C. was 6 feet, 9 inches tall—and asked him if he knew of Dr. Dobson.

A.C. looked at me warily. This wasn't the sort of question he usually received during post-game interviews.

"Yeah, I've heard of him," A.C. answered.

"Well, we're doing a story on guys who are willing to wait—willing to wait until marriage to have sex."

A.C.'s eyebrows peaked. I had his attention now.

"Is that something important to you—abstinence?" I asked.

"Oh, yes, that's something I talk about to kids all the time."

I had heard that A.C., who didn't hide his Christian faith under a bushel basket, hoped to become a preacher or a speaker when his playing days were over.

"But what does abstinence mean to *you*?" I probed.

"Oh, it's really important. I tell kids that abstinence works every time it's tried. Condoms aren't as successful as many would have you believe. Putting a condom on won't make you as secure as Fort Knox. Condoms have a hard enough time just stopping a woman from getting pregnant, let alone blocking the HIV virus. It's like water going through a net."

The way A.C. warmed to the subject matter told me that he had spoken a few times on this topic.

"But what does abstinence mean to *you*—in your life?" I wanted A.C. to talk about abstinence in personal terms, not just as something good and healthy for kids to practice.

A.C. skirted the question again and talked about how abstinence prevents unwanted pregnancy and helps stop the cycle of single-parent poverty.

When he was done, I made a show of clicking off the tape recorder and lowering my arm. "Sorry, A.C., but I kind of need to know something."

"What's that?"

"I need to know whether you're a virgin or not for this story."

A.C. looked me in the eyes and shrugged his shoulders. "Yeah, I am," he said matter-of-factly.

"Would you be willing to say that in *Focus on the Family* magazine?"

"Sure." This time A.C. didn't hesitate.

I explained how the process would work. I would interview him a little longer, and then I would write a story for him in the first person—as if *he* was the one who had written the article. Then I'd send him the article so he could make sure everything was expressed the way he wanted.

"Sounds great to me," A.C. said.

The Lakers forward gave me a great interview, and I returned to Colorado Springs and began writing right away. A few days later, I faxed a thousand-word story to the Lakers' team hotel in Philadelphia. When A.C. called me later, he made very few changes.

Here's an excerpt of what he had to say:

> *As a professional athlete, I have to deal with group-ies in many cities. It seems as though my teammates and I are often confronted by young women want-ing to meet us from the time we arrive to the time we depart. They hang out everywhere—airports, hotel lobbies, restaurants, and sports arenas—always try-ing to catch our eyes.*
>
> *Not many resist their advances. I don't know how many virgins there are in the NBA, but you can probably count them on one hand. Pro basket-ball players have this larger-than-life image, and it doesn't help when a former player such as a Wilt Chamberlain boasts about bedding twenty thou-sand women in his lifetime.*
>
> *While I've remained sexually pure, I still hear the locker room talk about the latest sexual con-quests. But I don't let that weaken my resolve be-cause I have chosen to follow God's standard. I've communicated my stand to my teammates. Some—in a humorous vein—have threatened to set me up with women who would make themselves available to me. "Let's see how strong you really are," they joke.*

We put a warm, engaging close-up picture of A.C. hug-ging a leather NBA basketball on the cover of the June 1993 issue, and we got great responses to the story. In fact, the A.C. Green-is-a-virgin story seemed to grow legs of its own, as other national magazines and big-city newspapers published their own articles about A.C.'s amazing decision.

Imagine that—being an NBA player, single to boot, and choosing not to have sex!

In 1999, after fifteen seasons in the NBA, A.C. received another shot of publicity as he neared the record for playing the most professional basketball games without a miss— 1,041, set by Ron Boone, who established the record playing in the American Basketball Association and the NBA. He was about to become the Cal Ripken of his sport.

But as *Sports Illustrated's* Rick Reilly pointed out, there was a much more impressive streak that A.C. had put together— remaining a virgin for thirty-six years.

"The NBA Player Who Never Scored" was the title of Reilly's column, and it was very complimentary and in good fun, which was nice to see in a national magazine. Here are some hilarious quips from a clever writer:

- "He's still as pure as a baby's sneeze."
- "He has lugged his morals in and out of every Hyatt from Sodom to Gomorrah."
- "Not only is Green perhaps the only adult virgin in the Los Angeles Basin, but he's kept his virginity while working in the NBA—the world's oldest permanent floating orgy! I mean, if you were trying to lose weight, would you spend fifteen years working at Häagen-Dazs? If you were an alcoholic, would you marry a Seagram's heir?"

A.C. played one more season in the NBA, extending his league record for consecutive games played to 1,192 before he retired following the 2000–01 season. He left behind a wonderful legacy.

When *Sports Illustrated* published its once-a-year "Where Are They Now?" issue in the summer of 2008, an article about him stated that when people heard the name A.C. Green, the word that sprung to mind most often, seven years after his retirement, was one not often associated with pro athletes: *virgin*.

"I love that people remember me for that," A.C. said. "I took a stand, and I was a voice for a generation. I'm proud of that."

MAKING A DIFFERENCE

A.C. Green's days as an NBA basketball player have been over for more than a decade, but his boldness in speaking up for biblical values means he was playing with purpose during all those years he chased loose balls and grabbed rebounds. Today, there are dozens of NBA players following in A.C.'s footsteps—trying to make a difference in the lives of those around them and in the lives of the fans looking on.

I'll be telling you about some of those players (and some other important people in the NBA) in *Playing with Purpose: Basketball.* They've agreed to share their stories because, like A.C. Green, they want their playing careers to count for something more than championship rings, individual awards, and hefty paychecks.

It's not an easy gig, playing in the NBA. The 82-game regular season schedule has players bouncing from city to city like a pinball. The physical strain of playing on back-to-back nights in different cities fatigues the legs and zaps the desire to perform at the highest level. Even the best-conditioned athletes find they must pace themselves during the season—even during games—so they have something in reserve for a fourth-quarter rally.

I would argue that Christian hoopsters have it even tougher in the NBA because of temptations that bombard them daily. They are regularly presented with every opportunity to turn *away* from Christ and *toward* themselves and the world.

These NBA players who follow Christ face challenges and temptations most of us can't even begin to understand. They have money and lots of free time on their hands . . . and they have flocks of women hoping to catch their eyes in hotel lobbies, restaurants, and bars.

The ladies are attractive and dressed provocatively, and they flirt like schoolgirls as they give the players their "come-hither" gazes. Some, unfortunately, are just looking to get pregnant by an NBA player. They see having an NBA star's child out of wedlock as a fast-track ticket to child-support payments that begin in the five figures and can rise to sums of $75,000 *a month*. The number of children NBA players father outside of marriage is staggering—and commonplace in other professional sports, too. Child support payments are some athletes' single biggest expense.

One of the players featured in this book told me the NBA has sent representatives out to talk to players about how to be "careful."

"They basically told us how to cheat and get away with it," he said. "It was pretty crazy. They told us to get a prepaid cell phone not registered in our name and not to leave any phone or text messages. They reminded us that if you have unprotected sex and knock up a girl, there are consequences, especially in New York City, where the state of New York will hit you with an alimony bill of $75,000 a month if you make the league average of $5 million. They reminded us that there are girls out for your money, so take precautions."

"Most people forget that we're talking about kids in their early twenties," said Jeff Ryan, the chaplain for the Orlando Magic. "If you can remember your early twenties, and I can remember mine, you don't always make the right choices. I was fortunate that I didn't have the temptations that these guys have. Remember, they are targeted. Some handle it well, and some don't. Unfortunately, there are plenty of guys who get caught up in the women thing and get their heads turned. They come into the league with the best of intentions, wanting to be faithful, wanting to be strong, but they give in to temptation. It's like my doctor telling me what I shouldn't eat. Once in a while I'm going to have it anyway. I think that's what happens to a lot of these guys. They know they shouldn't, but they give in."

Despite the threat of paternity suits, sexually transmitted diseases, and the emptiness associated with love-'em-and-leave-'em one-night stands, the easy availability of women sends many NBA players down a path "like an ox going to the slaughter, like a deer stepping into a noose," as Solomon, the wisest man who ever lived, wrote in Proverbs 7:22. We need to pray for those in the NBA who are staying strong—the A.C. Greens of today—as well as for those who know or have heard the Truth but are now living prodigal lives.

That's why I've written this book. Sure, I want to give you—the reader—interesting stories about some of the people in the NBA who are "playing with purpose" (or helping others to play with purpose). But I also want to give you the opportunity to support these talented athletes as they work to make their NBA careers a platform for taking the message of Jesus Christ to their teammates and the world around them.

Because as big and strong as they are on the basketball court, they need to be even *stronger* off the court.

1

DR. JAMES NAISMITH:
INVENTING WITH PURPOSE

The man who invented the game of basketball embraced Jesus Christ.

That's right. Dr. James Naismith, basketball's founder, was also a Christian theologian who invented the game more than a century ago as a way to reconcile his love of sports with Christian integrity.

Dr. Naismith had an amazing backstory that shows the hand of God directing his path. Born in 1861 near Almonte, Ontario, in Canada, James was the eldest son of Scottish immigrants John and Margaret Naismith. At the age of eight, James moved with his family to Grand-Calumet, Quebec, where his father began working as a sawhand at a lumber mill. The young boy would discover tragedy a year later when his parents both contracted typhoid fever. They died within three weeks of each other, leaving James and three younger brothers and sisters as orphans.

The reeling children were taken in by a godly grand-mother who lived in the east Ontario village of Bennies Corners, but then *she* died two years later. A bachelor uncle, Peter Young, gave them a home, but he was an authoritarian type who kept James busy around the farm and working in the woods. Young taught the boy how to chop trees, saw logs, and drive horses. His stern uncle put great stock in reliability and self-reliance, and he raised James and his siblings in God's Word.

James attended grade school in a one-room schoolhouse. The walk from the farm to school was five miles—and yes, the Canadian lad walked through snowdrifts in winter. James wasn't a great student but showed excellent hand-eye coordination and athletic skill. During the winter, his favor-ite activities were snowshoeing, skating, ice hockey, and tobogganing.

After the snow melted, James loved playing a simple children's game known as "duck on a rock." Players formed a line at a distance of fifteen to twenty feet from a base stone. Atop the stone was placed a smaller drake stone—otherwise known as the "duck." Each player would toss a fist-sized stone toward the "duck," attempting to knock the rock from its perch. Players found that the best way to play "duck on a rock" was to lob a soft shot rather than making a straight, hard throw. That's because if they missed, they had to retrieve their rock to stay in the game. So players found it better to throw their stones in an arc, a discovery that later proved essential in James' invention of basketball.

James attended Ontario's Almonte High School for two

years but dropped out to work as a logger in a lumber camp so he could help support his younger siblings. Life as a lumberjack meant hard—and dangerous—work. Then, at nineteen years of age, a random exchange altered the course of James' life. Here's the story:

James walked into a crowded bar and ordered a whiskey from the barkeep. A man standing at the bar, cap pulled low over his eyes, spoke to the young man without turning his head.

"Ye're Margaret Young's son, aren't ye?" he asked, using James' mother's maiden name.

"Aye," Naismith replied, reaching for his tumbler of whiskey.

"She'd turn over in her grave to see ye."

Naismith set the whiskey down—never to drink again. The story goes that he made a vow that night never again to do anything he knew would make his mother ashamed of him.

James realized that education was his only way out of a life of backbreaking, dangerous manual labor. He returned to high school, where a teacher named Thomas B. Caswell took an interest in his welfare and tutored him in reading, writing, arithmetic, Latin, and other subjects.

Naismith turned out to be a late bloomer academically, graduating from high school when he was twenty-one years old. After graduation, he immediately enrolled at McGill University in Montreal, where he was a rare four-sport athlete, competing in football, lacrosse, gymnastics, and rugby. James was a tough and durable athlete who rarely missed a game, match, or meet.

Naismith planned to go into the ministry, based upon his ideal for Christian service and honoring the memory of his mother. But many of his fellow students openly wondered how a future "man of the cloth" could justify his participation on football and rugby teams that attracted such bullies and brutes. Rugby and football—especially in those pre-Leatherheads days—were rough-and-tumble sports. Think *Gladiator* without the swords.

In the 1880s, many Christians believed that athletics were not only a waste of time but also a "tool of the devil." A group of James' friends—as well as his sister Annie—even met to pray for his soul. When Annie confronted her brother about his involvement in athletics, she cited Luke 9:62 ("Jesus replied, 'No one who puts a hand to the plow and looks back is fit for service in the kingdom of God'") as biblical proof that James should be in the pulpit, not the play yard.

Naismith didn't see things that way, though. In fact, this offspring of Scottish parents was a forerunner of Eric Liddell, the early twentieth-century Scottish athlete featured in the movie *Chariots of Fire.* Liddell said he could feel God's pleasure when he was sprinting because he was truly using the gifts God had given him. (By the way, Liddell also played the "brutish" game of rugby and later served as a Christian missionary to China.)

Naismith viewed athletics as a ministry and a way to impact others for Christ, a position that was strengthened after a telling incident involving a teammate on the rugby team. One time at practice, the teammate blurted a curse word in frustration. He looked up and noticed James had been within earshot. He knew of James' faith in Christ, and he immediately apologized to him.

"Sorry about that, Jim," said the offending player. "Forgot you were here."

Naismith had heard much worse language when he worked in the lumber camps, but on that day he realized that a righteous man could have an incredible impact on the athletic field, which, in those days, was mainly populated by ruffians.

After earning his bachelor's degree in physical education, Naismith stayed at McGill University and enrolled at Presbyterian College, McGill's theological school on the university campus, to earn his divinity degree. He kept playing on the football and rugby teams, which prompted more mumbling from Annie and from his theology professors. They must have really gotten their knickers in a knot after Naismith showed up in the student pulpit one Sunday morning sporting two black eyes earned in a particularly rough rugby match against Ottawa.

Naismith could not understand why so many people believed that his studying to be a minister disqualified him from playing and enjoying athletic competition. His belief was reinforced when a man from Yale University, an American named Amos Alonzo Stagg, appeared at McGill to deliver a lecture that said, in part, that it took many of the same qualities to become a good athlete as it did to become a good Christian, including enthusiasm, perseverance, and hard work.

It all came together for Naismith. He persevered and earned his divinity degree in 1890 from Presbyterian College and then moved to the United States, where he became both a graduate student and a PE instructor at the International YMCA Training School in Springfield, Massachusetts. The YMCA, as in the Young Men's Christian Association.

The "Gay Nineties" of the late nineteenth century was a time when the *C* in YMCA meant something more than just another letter in a Village People song. The Young Men's *Christian* Association was founded in 1844 in London, England, by a twenty-three-year-old fellow named George Williams.

Williams was concerned about the lack of healthy activities in major cities for young men like himself, many of whom were drawn from rural areas to factory work in London during the height of the Industrial Revolution. They worked ten to twelve hours a day, six days a week in a bleak landscape of noisy factories, overcrowded tenement housing, and dangerous influences. Taverns and brothels were their only entertainment options.

Williams and eleven friends organized the first YMCA meeting as a refuge of Bible study and fellowship for young men seeking escape from the hazards of life on the London streets. The YMCA offered something unique for its time, and its openness to anyone and everyone dissipated the rigid lines separating English social classes. The goal of putting Christian principles into practice, Williams said, was achieved through developing "a healthy spirit, mind, and body." The YMCA system became known as "muscular Christianity" because it promoted the idea that a healthy body leads to a healthy Christian mind.

The YCMA concept quickly traveled across the Atlantic Ocean to North America, and the first YMCAs were established in the United States prior to the Civil War. The local Ys broke down social barriers and brought together different church denominations in the United States. It's noteworthy that in the patriarchal society of the nineteenth century, women and children were also invited to take part in the YMCA's popular programs as well as their physical fitness classes.

It was this milieu that James Naismith became part of when he first arrived at the YMCA Training School, where he continued his athletic career by playing on the school's first football team, which was under the direction of none other than Amos Alonzo Stagg.

As a graduate student teacher, Naismith was given a group of restless college students who were taking a regular PE class during the winter quarter—presumably to burn off some energy and stay in shape until the spring lacrosse season. All students at the YMCA Training School were required to exercise for one hour a day—in keeping with the YMCA ideal—but there wasn't much for them to do during the winter other than march around the gym, perform jumping jacks, count off pushups, and do more monotonous calisthenics. These unpopular calorie-burning activities were pale substitutes for intramural football in the fall and lacrosse games in the spring.

Naismith did the best he could to keep enthusiasm high inside the school's gym that first winter. The following fall, he returned for his second year of graduate school, studying under Dr. Luther Halsey Gulick, the superintendent of physical education at the college. In one class called the Psychology of Play, Gulick stressed the need for a new indoor game that could be played during the winter months—a game that would be interesting to play and easy to learn.

As the fall semester came to a close, no one in Naismith's class had followed up on Gulick's challenge to invent such a game. Dr. Gulick pulled Naismith off to the side. He reminded James that football season was ending soon and that the young men at the YMCA Training School faced another dull winter of boring jumping jacks, uninspiring push-ups, and silly lines of leapfrog inside the gym.

"Naismith, I want you to see what you can do with those students," the superintendent said. "They need something that will appeal to their play instincts."

With those marching orders, Naismith went to work and came up with a checklist. Since the new game would be played in the winter, it had to be designed for the indoors. It also had to involve a large number of players and provide plenty of lung-burning exercise. Finally, since the game would be played in a confined space on a hardwood floor, it would have to forgo the roughness found in football, soccer, and rugby.

James also decided the sport could not be fundamentally elitist, like golf and tennis were at the time, nor could it require money for joining a country club or the purchase of expensive equipment. At its very heart, it must be a simple game—one for the masses, not just for the well-to-do.

Over the course of a couple weeks, Naismith took a little bit of this and a little bit of that from games already in existence:

- passing—from American rugby
- the jump ball—from English rugby
- the use of a goal—from lacrosse
- the size and shape of the ball—from soccer
- and the "shooting" of the ball toward a target— from his childhood game "duck on a rock"

Naismith approached the school janitor to ask if he could provide two eighteen-inch-square boxes to use as goals in the new game. The janitor rummaged around the storage room and found two peach baskets instead. Naismith nailed the half-bushel baskets to the lower rail of the gymnasium balcony, one at each end. The height of that lower balcony happened to be ten feet, which is where we get our ten-foot basket today. (Good thing the lower balcony wasn't *twelve* feet off the ground, or we wouldn't have the NBA Slam Dunk Contest every year.)

A man was stationed at each end of the balcony to pick the ball from the basket and put it back into play after a score. (It wasn't until a few years later that someone came up with the idea of cutting off the bottom of the peach baskets.) Naismith used a soccer ball for the game, and play involved running and passing to teammates—including the "bounce pass"—but no tackling. Dribbling was not part of the original game, but leather balls at that time weren't very symmetrical anyway, so they probably wouldn't have bounced consistently. The game's objective was for players to get the ball close enough to their elevated goal to toss it into the peach basket—and to prevent their opponents from doing the same to *their* goal.

Dr. Gulick was impressed with Naismith's new game, and he underlined the game's noble origins of fair play and no hard contact, lest a "foul" be called. He told Naismith, "The game must be kept clean. It is a perfect outrage for an institution that stands for Christian work in the community to tolerate not merely ungentlemanly treatment of guests, but slugging and that which violates the elementary principles of morals . . . therefore excuse for the rest of the year any player who is not clean in his play."

Naismith drew up thirteen original rules (see sidebar, next page) and published them on January 14, 1892, in the YMCA Training School newspaper, *The Triangle*.

THE 13 RULES OF BASKETBALL
by James Naismith

Author's note: This list of rules is the sturdy foundation that the game of basketball was laid upon 120 years ago. Of course, dozens of rules have been added to the game since then:

1. The ball may be thrown in any direction with one or both hands.

2. The ball may be batted in any direction with one or both hands, but never with the fist.

3. A player cannot run with the ball. The player must throw it from the spot on which he catches it, allowance to be made for a man running at good speed.

4. The ball must be held by the hands. The arms or body must not be used for holding it.

5. No shouldering, holding, pushing, striking or tripping in any way of an opponent. The first infringement of this rule by any person shall count as a foul; the second shall disqualify him until the next goal is made or, if there was evident intent to injure the person, for the whole of the game. No substitution shall be allowed.

6. A foul is striking at the ball with the fist, violations of Rules 3 and 4 and such as described in Rule 5.

7. If either side makes three consecutive fouls, it shall count as a goal for the opponents (consecutive means without the opponents in the meantime making a foul).

8. A goal shall be made when the ball is thrown or batted from the grounds into the basket and stays there, providing those defending the goal do not touch or disturb the goal. If the ball rests on the edges, and the opponent moves the basket, it shall count as a goal.

9. When the ball goes out of bounds, it shall be thrown into the field and played by the first person touching it. In case

of dispute, the umpire shall throw it straight into the field. The thrower-in is allowed five seconds. If he holds it longer, it shall go to the opponent. If any side persists in delaying the game, the umpire shall call a foul on them.

10. The umpire shall be the judge of the men and shall note the fouls and notify the referee when three consecutive fouls have been made. He shall have power to disqualify men according to Rule 5.

11. The referee shall be the judge of the ball and shall decide when the ball is in play, in bounds, to which side it belongs, and shall keep the time. He shall decide when a goal has been made and keep account of the goals, with any other duties that are usually performed by a referee.

12. The time shall be two fifteen-minute halves, with five minutes rest between.

13. The side making the most goals in that time shall be declared the winner.

And that's how Dr. James Naismith invented basketball.

The first game was played on January 20, 1892, at the YMCA Training School between two nine-player teams. The final score was 1–0; only one goal was made, a 25-foot shot that nestled inside the peach basket. You could say the players hadn't honed their shooting touch yet.

Despite the lack of scoring, the new game was an instant success. "Basket Ball" spread across the nation like wildfire as students who learned the game from Naismith took it across the country . . . and even around the world on Christian missions trips. Dozens of YMCAs and colleges around the country jumped on the basketball bandwagon and organized teams.

One of Naismith's protégés formed the first college team

at Geneva College in Beaver Falls, Pennsylvania. On April 8, 1893, Geneva defeated the New Brighton YMCA 3–0 in its first game. The first women's game was played at Smith College later that year. To this day, Geneva College is considered the birthplace of college basketball.

But this was all just the beginning. Over the coming decades, *basketball*, as the game came to be known, would change, grow, and expand into a game played all over the world and as a multi-billion-dollar enterprise.

DR. NAISMITH'S LEGACY: PLAYING THE GAME WITH PURPOSE

If you could travel back in time to January 20, 1892, and see the world's first basketball game, you'd probably see a sport that bears only a faint resemblance to the game as it is played today. On the other hand, if Dr. James Naismith could somehow appear at an NBA arena today—or even a high school or college gymnasium—he would probably have a hard time making a connection between the simple game he invented and the modern game of basketball.

There's no way Dr. Naismith could have envisioned the game of basketball as we know it today. He had no idea that the game would evolve into what it has become, just as he had no idea what kind of ball-handling, passing, and shooting skills players would develop over many decades.

It's impossible to say with certainty what parts of today's game would please Dr. Naismith and what parts would send him running to the exits. He would probably enjoy the teamwork and fundamentals, but it's probably safe to say he would have no use for the hot-dogging and showboating so many players have made a part of their game.

But we can also assume Dr. Naismith would recognize that there are young men and women today who use the game of basketball not just to enjoy the team atmosphere and the athletic compettion it provides—or, in rare cases, to make a king's ransom for playing a kid's game—but also to use it as a platform to share their faith in Jesus Christ and to make a difference in the world today.

In other words, Dr. Naismith would see that there are young athletes today who really are *playing with purpose.*

And, as a man of faith in and devotion to Jesus Christ, he'd be very pleased.

2

KYLE KORVER:
THE KNOCK-DOWN SHOOTER
WHO'LL KNOCK YOUR SOCKS OFF

You probably didn't know that Kyle Korver started a fashion trend in the NBA—wearing his socks long and high.

Kyle isn't going retro and bringing back the calf-high tube socks popular in the 1970s—the big-hair days when long-limbed players wore short, tight, bun-hugging shorts that showed a lot of leg. What Kyle wears are extra-long socks that cover his *entire* lower leg, all the way up to the knee, where they meet up with his baggy shorts. Lately, though, he's been showing a little knee.

Kyle, who's a come-off-the-bench-and-light-it-up scoring machine for the Chicago Bulls, started pulling his socks up to his kneecaps back in college. He has kept his socks up—as well as his long-range shooting skills—throughout a solid nine-year NBA career.

Blessed with the good looks of a Hollywood leading man, Kyle has disappointed a few female fans who'd like to see his gams. One time when he was playing for the Utah Jazz, two girls brought a homemade sign to the arena that said: HEY KORVER, SHOW US SOME LEG.

So how did the socks-to-the-knee fashion statement happen?

"When I was playing at Creighton University my sophomore year, a teammate said, 'Let's wear long socks tonight,' and I was, 'Okay, let's do it,'" Kyle explained. "And then I played a good game, so I wore long socks the next time we played, tucking the top underneath my knee pads. I had another good game, so I kept wearing them. It's become such a habit that if I play basketball *without* my long socks, I feel kind of naked.

"I take a lot of grief for wearing them, however, especially on the road. Fans ride me all game long, yelling things like 'Take your tights off!' or 'Give your girlfriend her socks back!' Between that and 'Ashton Kutcher,' I hear stuff like that all game long. But it's all in good fun. I learned to block it all out a long time ago."

Since you brought up Ashton Kutcher . . .

Do you see a resemblance between Kyle's facial features—the shock of tousled brown hair falling down his forehead, the high cheekbones, and the winning smile—and the Hollywood actor best known for marrying Demi Moore, fifteen years his senior, for replacing Charlie Sheen on *Two and a Half Men*, and for hosting the MTV hidden camera/practical joke series *Punk'd*? Many do, although Kyle doesn't see much of a resemblance. The only thing he and Ashton Kutcher have in common, he says, is that they both grew up in Iowa.

The celebrity lookalike thing is a cross Kyle must bear. He's given up telling kids on the street that he's not the Hollywood star they think he is, but if the teenyboppers insist on the actor's autograph, he scribbles a signature on a piece of paper so they can walk away happy. "I've been called Ashton Kutcher so many times that I've stopped counting," he said. "It's not that I have anything against him, but when you hear someone yell 'Ashton!' or 'You got punk'd!' for the fortieth game in the row, it gets pretty old."

What hasn't gotten old is seeing a high-arc jumper from beyond the three-point line whistle through the net. Kyle gets to see that a lot because he is one of the best spot-up, long-range shooters in the game today. "Shooting is what I do best," he said. "It'll always be what I do best."

Good thing, because filling up the basket is a great skill for an NBA player to have. His father, Kevin Korver, always told him, "If you can shoot, some team will need you."

As a potent perimeter threat throughout his NBA career, Kyle has made 41 percent of his three-point tries from beyond the 23-foot, 9-inch arc (22 feet from the corner sidelines) and 88 percent of his free throws. He holds the NBA season record for highest three-point shooting percentage with an amazing 53.6, set during the 2009–10 season with the Utah Jazz. He has also led the league in free throw shooting during the 2006–07 season with 91.4 percent.

Kyle isn't a starter for the Bulls, but he's expected to come in cold off the bench, spell the starters, and keep the offense going. At 6 feet, 7 inches tall, he usually plays the position of shooting guard—of course—but he can also play small forward.

The key to being a great role player is knowing what your

job is and not trying to be the star—a supporting role that suits Kyle well. Not only does he play tough defense, dive for loose balls, and find the open man, but he can be counted on to make the clutch shots in crunch time—which is why he's often left in the game late in the fourth quarter.

Kyle plays unselfishly and has great chemistry with his teammates, and he's one of the reasons the Chicago Bulls had such a great 2010–11 season.

There's another reason Kyle plays unselfishly, as you'll soon learn.

SPECIAL K'S

If you want a quick description of what Kyle's life was like growing up, try this: it was pretty much church and basketball. His father was a pastor, just like *his* father before him, so Kyle almost literally grew up in the church. As for the basketball side, both his parents are crazy about the game and played it at the collegiate level.

Kevin Korver was quite a player, making a name for himself in the mid-1970s at Central College in Pella, Iowa, where he twice won the Mentink Award for leadership, sportsmanship, and inspiration. His mother, Laine, was no slouch on the hardwood, either. She once scored 74 points in a high school game, and if you're wondering how that's possible in a thirty-two-minute contest, here's the explanation:

When Laine grew up in Iowa, high school girls' teams played six-on-six basketball.

Six-on-six?

"In six-on-six basketball, you don't get to cross the half-court line, so there are three players on defense and three on offense," Kyle said. "The whole goal of six-on-six basketball was to pick up the pace of the game. Mom played on the offensive side of the court, so it was three-on-three basketball. She was their main scorer, averaging something like 43 or 44 points a game her junior year. She used to put up some pretty big numbers."

Kevin and Laine met at Central College's admissions office, where they both worked. They fell in love and eventually married. Following graduation, Kevin, no doubt influenced by the career path of his father, Harold Korver, who was a minister in the Reformed Church of America, felt the Lord calling him into the ministry.

Kyle's grandfather grew up as one of eight kids on an Iowa farm during the Great Depression of the 1930s. There wasn't much food on the table during those Dust Bowl days, but somehow Harold and his family survived. Their hard-scrabble existence—the family lived without electricity and indoor plumbing—shaped Harold's character. As a young man, he decided that he wanted to labor in the fields for a different kind of harvest—souls for the Kingdom. He became a church pastor in Iowa, but in 1971 he accepted the pastorate of Emmanuel Reformed Church and moved his family of five sons (Kevin was the oldest) to Paramount, California, a Los Angeles suburb.

Paramount is south of downtown Los Angeles—as in south-central LA. Back in the 1970s, Paramount was a tough, blue-collar community cut from the same tattered cloth as nearby Bellflower, Compton, Lakewood, and Lynwood. Kevin attended Paramount High School, where he was a basketball standout. Following his graduation from high school, he returned to his Iowa roots by playing for Central College, a Christian college affiliated with the Reformed Church of America. Harold Korver had graduated from Central College in 1952.

Shortly after Kevin married Laine, his father asked him to come back to Paramount to help him minister to families in a community ravaged by drugs and hopelessness. The young couple readily agreed to start their lives together in Southern California. Kevin joined his brother Ken as an assistant pastor at Emmanuel.

Kyle, the oldest of four sons, was born in 1981 in Paramount. (His brothers are named Klayton, Kaleb, and Kirk . . . as you'll see throughout this chapter, the Korver family has this K thing going.) The family lived in a parsonage, a church-provided home where pastors and their families live to offset the high cost of housing. "I doubt anyone knows what a parsonage is today," Kyle said, "but that was our home."

One day when Kyle was four or five years old, he watched his uncle Kris play in a high school basketball game. (Kris was fifteen years younger than his brother Kevin.) "I remember sitting in the stands, looking down on the court and thinking, *Wow, how cool would that be to be on that court in front of all these people who've come to watch me play,*" Kyle said. "I loved all the cheering, excitement, and competition. I couldn't grasp it all at that age, but there was something about basketball that made me think, *I want to be on that court someday.*"

Kyle started playing hoops at the church playground, where basketball rims and backboards had been erected over an asphalt playing surface. There were always kids to play with after school and on weekends. Kyle would practice for hours on that court, pretending he was Magic Johnson and hearing Lakers' radio announcer Chick Hearn in his mind:

Rebound from Kareem to Magic. It's a three-on-two. Magic into the middle. He's still going. Looking left . . . great fake . . . lays it up and in!

Magic yo-yoing with the ball, puts McHale into the pop-corn machine, dribble drive, hangs Bird out to dry—alley-oop is good!

Magic's "Showtime" with the Lakers was in full bloom when Kyle entered elementary school. "I watched the Lakers a lot on TV during the basketball season," Kyle said. "We did not have a whole lot of money growing up, so we could never afford to go to a Lakers game. But we would watch the Lakers on TV every chance we got."

Kyle joined a basketball league in the third grade that played on Saturday mornings. Sundays were reserved for church, but that didn't mean he couldn't go out and play after the services let out. There were times when Kyle and his friends would head out to the asphalt court and play in their Sunday best, trying not to get their nice clothes dirty.

One time, Kyle was shooting baskets with two hands when his uncle Kris dropped by. "That's pretty good, but you have to pick a hand to shoot with—right or left," the elder Korver said.

Kyle was right-handed, but for some reason, he could shoot the ball farther with his left hand. After the word of advice from Uncle Kris, he started shooting with his left hand. This went on for a good year until his uncle saw him shooting jumper after jumper with his *left* hand. When Uncle Kris asked him why he was shooting left-handed, Kyle answered, "You told me to pick a hand, so I picked my left."

"Well, you're right-handed, so you should use your other hand," Uncle Kris said, knowing that Kyle would be more coordinated—and more accurate—using his dominant hand. So that's what Kyle did. But all that practicing with his left hand helped him develop greater ball-handling skills. "Even today when I pass the ball, I'm apt to do it with my left hand and not my right," he said.

Since the family lived across the street from the church, they had planted themselves into the heart of a struggling community. In 1980, Paramount residents were shocked when their community was named the fourth-worst U.S. city (with a population under fifty thousand) to live in. The negative publicity prompted the Korver pastors to launch an Emmanuel Reformed Church campaign called "Let's Get Paramount's Neighborhoods Looking Good Again."

During the campaign, every other Saturday, the church would supply a couple of hundred volunteers, and the city would provide the supplies and public works supervisors to guide the small army of workers. Together they would clean up trash, landscape yards, haul away overgrowth, and paint over graffiti. Kyle, just eight years old at the time, found out that he could be handy with a paintbrush and could also make himself useful by picking up trash.

"We transformed the entire city that summer and fall," he said. "I can remember painting over the graffiti on those walls, though, and then coming back two weeks later and seeing graffiti there again. We would paint over it a second or a third or a fourth time. Eventually, the taggers got tired of doing the graffiti because they knew we would paint over it again. People took pride in themselves and how their neighborhood looked. We saw an overall attitude change. Gangs were no longer welcome, and crime rates dropped. Sure, our helping hands, some paint, and a positive attitude helped, but it really was about love. Our church received a Point of Light Award from President Bush."

Helping out the Paramount community on Saturday mornings taught Kyle a valuable lesson: "The whole concept of serving others was ingrained into my head at a young age. I was taught by my parents that it's just what you do."

CHANGES AHEAD

While Kyle was learning about what it meant to serve others, a couple of things happened to shake up his orderly world. They both occurred when he was in the fifth grade, although at that age he wasn't able to really understand the full context of what was going on in the adult world around him.

The first incident happened on a weekday in November 1991, and Kyle remembers like it was yesterday.

"I came home from school, and Mom met me at the door," Kyle said. "She was crying. I asked what was wrong, and she explained that Magic had AIDS and couldn't play basketball anymore. I was so sad. I did not totally understand what AIDS or HIV was, but I just knew that he was really sick and would never play basketball again."

The other incident affected the community Kyle and his family lived in far more seriously. In the spring of 1992, a bystander videotaped the beating of a black motorist named Rodney King, who had been stopped following a high-speed pursuit. When an all-white jury acquitted four white police officers, the verdict provoked fury in the predominantly black neighborhoods of south-central Los Angeles. Over a six-day period, widespread looting, assault, arson, and murder erupted in the gritty urban areas that surrounded Paramount.

Kyle remembers seeing, from his bedroom window, flames and smoke rise into the sky. Storefronts were burning in Compton, which bordered Paramount, and looters ransacked retail outlets. At one point, a mob dragged a white truck driver from his vehicle and beat him severely as news helicopters circled above, recording the incident.

Soon after the riots, Kyle's father did a preaching series on the book of Jonah to encourage the congregation to be a people of faith who were willing to enter into a city that seemed to be disintegrating.

"Shortly after I preached on that topic, we received a phone call from Iowa," Kevin said. "The Third Reformed Church in Pella asked me to become their pastor. This was totally out of the blue and threw me for such a loop that my back gave out. The anticipation all along was that we would become the senior pastor family of Emmanuel Reformed Church. Our congregation in Paramount seemed to be affirming it. This is what I knew and was trained for—inner-city ministry. And yet we were being asked to move to small, rural, and white Iowa."

Kevin and Laine were the parents of four boys, all under the age of eleven. *Is this where God wants us to move the family?* they wondered. They were happy in Paramount and committed to staying for as long as God wanted them there. But as they prayed for direction and talked to family members, they sensed the Lord leading them to Third Reformed Church in Pella, where Kevin had lived before the move to California in 1971.

"When my parents told me that we were moving, I cried for a good month," Kyle said. "I did not want to leave. I was a California kid all the way. I liked the sunshine. I liked the beach. I liked being able to shoot baskets outside year-round. I didn't even have a pair of jeans at the time. I wore shorts to school every day and took pride in that. There were a lot of reasons why we moved, but I think my dad being obedient to the Lord's leading was the main reason."

In the mid-nineteenth century, about eight hundred Dutch immigrants founded Pella, now a small city of ninety-eight hundred in central Iowa. An annual Tulip Time Festival celebrates the town's Dutch heritage, but it is better known throughout the United States as the manufacturing home of the popular Pella windows, a company a Dutch couple founded in 1925.

Is everything starting to come together here? Korver is a Dutch name, and Kyle's family heritage could be traced to the immigrants who settled in Pella in the 1800s. Pella was home to them. The Reformed Church of America, their denomination, dated back to the Dutch colonists who settled New Amsterdam—later known as New York City—in the early 1600s. Third Reformed in Pella was a megachurch with twenty-five hundred members—this in a town of barely ten thousand people.

The Korvers would go from being small fish in the big pond of Paramount to a fishbowl existence in Pella.

"We were a big part of the community in Pella, as you can imagine," Kyle said. "When we moved back just before my teenage years, I definitely found out that there is a spotlight that comes with being a PK—a preacher's kid. Everyone was watching me, and I felt like I was supposed to act in a certain way. With a lot of pressure and a lot of eyes on me, I think my family did a good job of not forcing their faith on me or saying, *You have to be this way, you have to do that, you have to uphold the standard that makes us look good.* They were never that way with me or my brothers."

Kyle said his parents were smart in the way they raised him and his brothers. Since they were at church whenever the doors were open, they knew it would be easy to burn out their kids with youth group on Wednesday nights, Sunday school, church services on Sunday morning and Sunday evening, plus the special events that find their way onto the church calendar.

"If we had been in church for five nights in a row, for example, my parents would tell us on Sunday morning, 'We'll skip Sunday school this morning and just go to church,' or 'We won't go to Sunday night service.' There would be Sundays when my father wasn't preaching, and we would all stay home and not go to church. Maybe Dad would go through a Bible story with us at breakfast or talk a little longer at lunch, but he'd let us know that we were taking a break."

One of the first things Kyle and Laine did when they moved the family back to Pella was install a basketball court in the backyard of their new home. Bringing in dirt, laying down a concrete slab, putting in a basketball standard, and erecting lights cost two thousand dollars—not a trifling sum.

Kyle's father announced at dinner one night that if the family was going to spend that much on a basketball court, they should match the amount with a gift to charity. In other words, forget about going to Disney World next summer. His parents already had the same idea in place for Christmas— whatever they spent on gifts for themselves, they gave the same amount away so that the focus wasn't all about *getting*.

The boys didn't bat an eye. "That was the mind-set in which I was raised," Kyle said. "Everything was all about supporting the Lord's work and trusting God for your future."

During his middle school years, Kyle played for a team his uncle Karl coached. Uncle Karl schooled Kyle—the former California kid who tossed no-look passes and flipped scoop shots toward the rim—on meat-and-potatoes Midwest basketball fundamentals. No Showtime in Pella.

Kyle learned how to set and use screens, break a press, and run an offense from the point guard position. Wraparound, behind-the-back passes were out; chest-high two-handed passes were in. Kyle's passing game, jump shot, and fundamentals improved quickly and raised his game several notches, which helped him make the Pella High School varsity as a sophomore. Even though he was a great player in high school—the Dutch retired his No. 25 in 2006—he wasn't heavily recruited to play college basketball.

The best basketball school that recruited Kyle was Creighton University, a Catholic institution in Omaha, Nebraska, which was just 180 miles west of Pella. Being close enough to go home on weekends to see the family and enjoy Mom's cooking was a huge draw for Kyle. Plus, his parents and brothers could come to his home games. Kyle also liked the Midwest feel of Omaha, showing that his days as a California beach boy were finally behind him. (He still streaked his hair with blond surfer-dude highlights, though.)

As for the basketball side, Creighton may not have been a big-time program like Duke or North Carolina—but it was still Division I ball in the highly competitive Missouri Valley Conference, which gave flight to Larry Bird, by the way. Larry had played at Indiana State.

Kyle played a big part in bringing Creighton back to national prominence, leading the Bluejays into the NCAA Tournament—March Madness—all four of his seasons.

The highlight was the 2002–03 season, Kyle's senior year, when the Bluejays won 29 regular-season games. Creighton was consistently ranked in the Top 20 that season, and Kyle earned Missouri Valley Conference Most Valuable Player honors and was named an Associated Press Second Team All-American.

College basketball's three-point line was 19 feet, 9 inches from the basket when Kyle played for Creighton, and he made mincemeat of that standard. (The NCAA extended the three-point distance to 20 feet, 9 inches in 2007.) He made 371 career three-pointers at Creighton, which tied him for sixth in NCAA history, and shot 45.3 percent from long distance. In one game against Xavier, his shooting stroke accounted for *eight* three-pointers, and he hit seven in games against Notre Dame and Fresno State. Kyle was also invited to the Three-Point Shootout during the Final Four weekend, where he finished second out of eight competitors.

NBA scouts were there, notepads in hand.

As his father said, teams could always use another shooter.

A COLD DRINK AND A BOX OF DONUTS

Unlike the NFL, which constantly replenishes its teams with untested rookies drafted out of college, the NBA is more of a closed shop. It's not often that players taken after the first round of the NBA draft catch on with an NBA team. Teams can have up to fifteen players signed and practicing with them, but only twelve can suit up for games.

Kyle was an underrated player from what is considered a lesser conference going into the 2003 NBA draft. Would he go in the first round? After the end of Kyle's senior year, thirty guys crowded into his dorm room at Creighton to watch the draft unfold, ready to cheer when Kyle's name was called.

Kyle wasn't drafted in the first round, which put a damper on the party. As the second round progressed and his name was still not called, his dorm room resembled a tomb. With three draft picks left in the second round, ESPN cut to a commercial break. When NBA draft coverage resumed, Kyle's name was part of the "crawl" along the bottom of the screen. Cheers erupted! The New Jersey Nets had taken a flier on him in the second round, making him the fifty-first player picked.

Kyle began thinking how he'd get a chance to fulfill a dream that began on the asphalt courts back in Paramount, but then he learned the stunning news: after drafting him, the Nets immediately traded him to the Philadelphia 76ers—for "a cold drink and a box of donuts," he quipped.

Kyle caught on with the 76ers and showed he wasn't afraid to shoot the trey in the NBA. Early in the season, he came off the bench to connect on five-of-five three-pointers against Boston and started receiving more PT, or playing time. He was making it in the NBA. He was achieving his lifelong goal of playing before big crowds, traveling in style, staying in the best hotels, and receiving a handsome salary.

During Kyle's NBA rookie year, he was the only white player on the 76ers, so his teammates called him "Sunshine," the nickname of the long-haired white quarterback in the movie *Remember the Titans*. And as he continued to pour in jump shots from near the 76er bench, his teammates added another nickname: *Sniper*. "That was my street name, my street cred," Kyle said.

And yet, despite his acceptance, Kyle was unsettled. Something didn't feel right.

Near the end of his rookie season, Kyle woke up one morning feeling sick to his stomach. Why?

"Because I felt like I had totally missed the boat," he said. "I was like, *I am here, in the NBA. I can walk down the street and people want my autograph. I can walk into a mall, and if I see a hat or a shirt that I like, I can buy it because I have enough money. I don't have to look at the price tag.*

"These were the things that you think will make you happy. You have fame, people recognize you, people like you, people cheer for you, and I was sitting there at that moment feeling sick to my stomach. I felt that I had nothing in my life. I was wondering, *What is going on?*"

Kyle trudged from his bed to his shower. He lived in a huge apartment complex where the hot water never ran out. He stood in the shower for forty-five minutes, letting the water cascade over him as he grappled with heavy thoughts about the meaning of life and about his faith in Christ.

His faith, he knew in his gut, had been primarily based on keeping the rules, on staying within the boundaries. As long as he stayed inside the lines, he believed, he was right with God. At least that was how he had been living his life. But as he examined his soul, Kyle knew he wasn't fooling anybody. Sure, he wasn't a bad person and he wasn't doing anything illegal or crazy, but he wasn't pursuing his faith in the Lord. He had fallen into the trap of thinking that being a "good" person was enough. But it wasn't enough. God wanted his heart, soul, and mind—not his good works and his keeping a bunch of rules.

Kyle thought about how he had tried to find a good church. So far in Philadelphia, he hadn't had any luck. He quickly learned that the NBA doesn't base its weekly schedule around church and that he was much more likely to have a Sunday game (often a road game) than have Sunday off.

One Sunday, though, Kyle didn't have a game, so he decided to check out a Reformed Church that was on a list his father gave him. It was only four blocks from his apartment. One of his good friends from high school, Adam Bruckner, was living with Kyle, so off they went.

When the two young men walked into the church, the first thing Kyle saw was a huge map of Korea. Then he looked around, and all he saw were Koreans. He and Adam had walked into a Korean church! Kyle remembers how everyone welcomed him and Adam and insisted that they take a seat right up front. "I was by far the tallest man in church that day," he said. "I must have blocked people's vision for five rows behind me."

Okay, so the Korean church wasn't the right fit for him. His other attempts to find Christian fellowship in Philly had been air balls, too.

Kyle lowered himself to the shower floor as the warm water continued to wash over him. He poured out his heart to God: "Lord, I know there is more to life than this. I have seen it in my family. I have seen purpose in their lives, but basketball is not doing it for me. I need to get back on track. I may have been there at one time, but I'm not there now. I don't want this anymore. I want You to change my heart."

Then Kyle had a question burning within.

"God, why haven't You given me a church that I can regularly attend?"

Kyle sat there and cried as the water poured over his body, and then he heard a voice in the quiet of his heart.

Because you haven't asked Me.

Kyle stopped. It was true. He hadn't asked the Lord specifically for a church. So he closed his eyes and whispered this prayer: "Lord, I need a church. I need a community. I need people. I need worship. I need all these things. Please help me find a church."

And then the hot water finally ran out.

"Kind of a crazy story," Kyle said.

So what happened?

"A few days later, my roommate wanted to meet up with these girls at this bar, but I did not want to go there for a whole lot of reasons," Kyle said. "He said, 'I met this girl, and she was really cute. I need somebody to go with me.'

"'Dude, I don't want to come. I have a game tomorrow. I don't want to sit in a smoky bar.' But eventually he talked me into it. So I go, and I'm sitting in the corner, watching SportsCenter when these girls walk in. The girl wasn't cute and her friends weren't cute either. They sat and immediately lit up cigarettes, which I hated. Then I saw these two guys waving me over, so I excused myself to go over and talk to them."

The three made small talk, and the two men asked Kyle where he was from. "I told them my dad was a pastor, and they said, 'We're Christians, too.' So we started sharing our faith, and we ended up praying together in that bar. Then they said I had to come to their church. It was ten miles away with about seven hundred people our age. I said, 'You have to be kidding me.' "

And that's how God answered Kyle's prayer to find a church: Calvary Fellowship in Downingtown, Pennsylvania. The church held a Sunday night service called "The Bridge," and Kyle got himself plugged in right away.

"That was huge for me," he said. "After that prayer, it was like *wham!* I had community, church, spiritual leadership, accountability—all those things. I learned that you have to ask God for the desires of your heart and that God won't give you what you don't need. He will give you what you need if you just ask for it."

COAT DRIVE

A couple of good things happened after Kyle got plugged into a new church during his second season in the NBA:

1. He won a starting position with the 76ers.
2. He collected tons of coats on behalf of something called "Operation Warm."

Operation Warm provided new winter coats to children in need. The 76ers and the NBA hosted coat drives to collect the much-needed winter clothing. Early in his second year with the 76ers, the front office asked Kyle if he wanted to be part of Operation Warm and lead the coat drive—be the public face, if you will.

"At first, I didn't want to because the player who did it the previous year went through the locker room, hitting up teammates for money. He was like, 'Yo, rookie, give me two hundred bucks. I gotta buy coats for the kids.' I wanted to do more than ask my teammates for money, so I took a different approach. I had several coat drives before games and announced that anyone who brought a coat to the game could meet me, get an autograph, or have a picture taken with me. The coat drive ended up being a huge success and a really cool thing." When he was playing in Philadelphia, more than twenty-eight hundred coats were collected and given to needy families.

Operation Warm whetted Kyle's appetite to do more with his rising visibility as an NBA player. He started his own foundation—the Kyle Korver Foundation—and became its biggest donor.

Then another opportunity for ministry came his way. Here's how that happened:

"I was living downtown, and Adam and I were driving to Cavalry Fellowship, our church out in Downingtown. The trip could be an hour to three hours to get there, depending on whether there had been an Eagles game that day.

"One Sunday evening, we happened to start driving for Downingtown right after the end of an Eagles game. We were stuck in traffic for close to three hours. We were late for church, miserable, and asking ourselves, *Why are we driving to Downingtown when we live in downtown Philadelphia? How come there isn't a church we like closer to where we live?*

"So we kicked around the idea, *Why don't we start a church?* We knew what we wanted it to look like. We gave the idea some serious thought and prayer. We had a pretty strong sense from the Lord that something was going to happen.

"We talked to a bunch of people and got a small group together, and my friend Adam had run a homeless meal ministry downtown on Mondays for the last seven years. The place where he cooked his meals was called the Helping Hands Mission in North Philly. It wasn't a real good neighborhood, but that was the only place we could find to meet.

"So we started meeting there on Tuesday nights, just like a Bible study. We were sitting on the front steps of the mission one night, a bunch of us white people. The neighborhood kids came out. There was an apple tree close by, so they chucked a bunch of apples at us.

"We were trying to be good Christian people. I said, 'You guys are funny, but you better not throw any more apples in case we fire back.' I said it with a friendly smile that diffused the situation. A couple of weeks later, some guys in our group were throwing around a football when the neighborhood kids came running over and wanted to play. We started playing with them, and they talked some trash and we talked some trash back, and everyone had a good time. We had such a good time that when we came back the following week an hour early, the kids wanted to come out and play football with us.

"We started to come an hour early every single week. We learned their names, talked with them, and got to know them. We cleared it with the mission to bring the kids inside, where we did crafts and shared Bible stories."

That was the modest beginning of an after-school

program, which Adam runs to this day, that mentors kids, puts on basketball camps, and tutors them with their homework—all funded through the Kyle Korver Foundation.

"We've put up some really nice goal-centered hoops with fiberglass backboards that can be cranked up from six feet to ten feet," Kyle said. "There are eighteen of them put up all over the neighborhood. We have over a hundred kids coming every week, including Muslims. It's something great to be a part of."

BASKETBALL WITHOUT BORDERS

Kyle settled nicely into a starting role with Philadelphia, but in the middle of his fifth season in the league, he was traded to the Utah Jazz. Adam Bruckner remained in Philadelphia to run the inner-city after-school program.

After learning that Kyle was a God-fearing guy with a charitable heart, the fans in Salt Lake City embraced him, but they also appreciated how the team improved after his arrival. The Jazz had a so-so 16–16 record before Kyle joined the team in late 2007, but his silky-smooth shooting helped lift the Utah Jazz from ninth place to fourth in the NBA Western Conference standings as the Jazz won 38 of its last 50 games.

The "Korver Effect," as the media called it, carried over to the young women attending the sold-out games. Masha Kirilenko, the wife of Andrei Kirilenko, one of Kyle's new teammates, owned a boutique called *Fleur de Lis*, and she made a mint selling pink "Mrs. Korver" T-shirts to smitten female fans.

Kyle took it all in stride and looked for new ways to contribute off the court. He came up with an out-of-the-box idea:

support a nonprofit construction company that could build handicapped ramps for people in need. He asked his brother Klayton to give him a hand with the foundation work and to oversee an initiative to build wheelchair ramps as well as perform roof repairs and landscaping. "We've built almost forty ramps in 2011, but all this stuff obviously costs money," Kyle said.

Kyle donates plenty of his own money to his foundation work, but the need is great.

"We do fund-raisers, fun things like dodgeball and kickball tournaments, but we came up with an idea for a T-shirt line to raise money for the foundation," Kyle said. "A guy hooked us up with Hurley and other companies to get us going. We came up with sixteen T-shirts with really cool designs. They have a theme to them: Strength-Love, Strength-Courage, Strength-Courage-Honor, Peace, Respect, and Knowledge. What is Strength? Strength is not being the bully of the block. It's an inner strength and an inner confidence.

"We called our company 'Seer Clothing' because a seer in the Bible is a visionary or a prophet. Our website is SeerClothing.com, and everything we make after expenses goes straight into our foundation and our causes."

Finally, there's one more Kyle Korver story that needs to be mentioned, and it's his involvement with Basketball Without Borders, a joint effort of the NBA and the International Basketball Federation (FIBA) to promote the sport and encourage positive social change in the areas of education, health, and wellness in local communities.

During the first four off-seasons of his career, Kyle has volunteered to fly to China, Brazil, South Africa, and India to promote the game by working at a basketball camp in the morning with top junior players from each country and then doing some type of community project in the afternoon.

His last trip was to India during the summer of 2008 when he joined fellow NBA players Ronny Turiaf, Pat Garrity, Linton Johnson, and a team of NBA coaches for the league's first outreach event in India.

"I love to see the world because it gives me an incredible perspective on how life is outside the United States," Kyle said. "India was an incredible experience. I saw people bathing in front of fire hydrants, eating food with flies all over it, and renting out space on sidewalks so they could sleep at night. I had seen that stuff on *National Geographic* shows before I went, but when you go there and actually talk to people in the streets, it gives you a whole new perspective on life, especially for guys in the NBA.

"I mean, we are so fortunate. It's easy to take everything for granted, but life in many parts of the world is not like it is here in the United States. Going on the Basketball Without Borders trips helps keep my heart right."

That's great to hear, but Kyle's heart has been in the right place for a long time.

3

ANTHONY PARKER:
TAKING HIS GAME
WHERE JESUS WALKED

Like every American old enough to remember that day, Anthony Parker (not to be confused with Tony Parker, the French basketball player who plays for the San Antonio Spurs) will never forget where he was when he learned that terrorists had flown two passenger jets into the World Trade Center on September 11, 2001.

Anthony was in Tel Aviv, Israel, preparing for his second season with Maccabi Tel Aviv, one of the premier teams in European professional basketball. Around four o'clock in the afternoon (Israel is seven hours ahead of the Eastern Time Zone), Anthony was meeting his agent in Israel at a restaurant when he asked Anthony if he had heard the news about a plane hitting the World Trade Center in Manhattan.

"No, I haven't heard anything," Anthony replied. He

imagined a small private plane clipping one of the Twin Towers. His mind couldn't envision anything larger than that.

Anthony returned to his Tel Aviv apartment and flicked on CNN International. As he and his wife, Tamaris, watched the events of that day live, they were horrified by the incredible sight of the mighty Twin Towers collapsing one after another into a mountainous pile of rubble, dust, and debris. What Anthony witnessed that day shook his confidence—and tangibly reminded him that he was living in a Middle Eastern country where acts of terrorism happened often and occurred without warning.

He wondered if he had done the right thing by taking his game overseas. Since America had been hit by a massive terrorist attack, was Israel next? The question rolled around in Anthony's mind, and in those first few uncertain hours after four planes were hijacked in the United States, anything seemed possible. There were anxious moments that day and evening as he and Tamy tried to call loved ones back home in the United States but found their efforts fruitless because of the jammed telephone lines.

So how did this American basketball player find himself in Tel Aviv on that fateful day?

Anthony's story begins with his father, Larry, who was a good basketball player at the University of Iowa. Larry got to know his future wife, Sara, when she played on the intramural basketball team he coached. After they fell in love and married, the young couple went into the commercial insurance business and settled in Naperville, Illinois.

A few years ago, *Money* magazine ranked Naperville, a bucolic municipality of a hundred thousand, as the second-best small city in America. Naperville's close proximity to

Chicago and its popular Riverwalk brick path, which follows the DuPage River's course through downtown, makes this upper middle-class community a great place to raise a family.

Anthony, Larry and Sara Parker's first child, was born in 1975. Dad practically put a Nerf basketball in his hands while he was still in his crib. Before he started elementary school, young Anthony was practicing in the backyard on a Nerf basketball hoop with a picture of Julius Erving (Dr. J) on the backboard.

"My father was my main basketball influence and showed me how to play the game," Anthony said. "Dad played in men's leagues while I was growing up, and my earliest memories were going to his games, where I would run out onto the floor during halftime and try to throw the ball at the rim."

Anthony's parents were keen on his education, and the excellent Naperville school district was one reason why families flocked to live within its borders. Anthony grew like a tree sapling between his freshman and sophomore years at Naperville Central High, vaulting from 5 feet, 8 inches to 6 feet, 2 inches tall. His game also jumped by leaps and bounds, and he continued growing, reaching 6 feet, 5 inches by his senior year. He added another inch in college.

Though he was quite a player, Anthony's high school years weren't all basketball. Schoolwork and education were also important—more important than even his rising basketball skills. He excelled academically in math and science classes.

But Anthony worked hard on his game. You'd think that as a young man growing up in the Chicago area in the mid-1990s, Anthony would have idolized Michael Jordan, but he wasn't swept up by MJ fever. He was intent on honing his passing and shooting skills and becoming the *first* Anthony Parker, not the second coming of His Airness.

Anthony had the good grades and the basketball chops to play at many colleges, but he wanted to commit to a program early so that he wouldn't have to worry about losing a full-ride offer due to injury. He chose a private institution, Bradley University, because of its strong academic reputation, solid basketball tradition, and close proximity to home. Located in Peoria, Illinois, Bradley was just 150 miles from Naperville, meaning his parents would be close enough to attend most of his home games.

Larry and Sara Parker deserve a lot of credit for raising three children of accomplishment. Anthony's younger brother, Marcus, is a radiologist who graduated from Washington University in St. Louis and went on to medical school at Johns Hopkins University, where he also completed his residency. He's married and lives with his two little girls fifteen minutes from Anthony's permanent residence in Tampa, Florida.

And you may have heard of Anthony's youngest sibling, Candace. She happens to be one of the best female basketball players in the world.

BROTHER-SISTER ACT: ANTHONY AND CANDACE PARKER

She's the first Woman's National Basketball Association (WNBA) player to win the Most Valuable Player crown and Rookie of the Year award in the same season. She's also the first woman to dunk in an NCAA tournament game, which she did when she was a key member of the University of Tennessee's Lady Volunteers basketball team—winner of the 2007 and 2008

NCAA championships. She's also the second woman to dunk in a WNBA game.

We're talking about Candace Parker, Anthony's little sister—although at an eye-popping 6 feet, 4 inches tall, she's not that little. Candace dominates the game in a way few women have. On any night, she can be the best scorer, best passer, best guard, best forward, best post player, and best rebounder on the floor.

She's also a great mom. Candace married Shelden Williams, a college basketball star for Duke University who has played several seasons in the NBA, and the couple welcomed a girl, Lailaa Nicole Williams, into the world in 2009. Candace took maternity leave for the entire season, but now she's back playing for the Los Angeles Sparks in the WNBA as well as a Russian team, UMMC Ekaterinburg. She can afford a nanny: the Russian team pays her a reported $1.2 million annually.

So Anthony, was there any sibling rivalry between brother and sister growing up? Did you and Candace go at each other in cutthroat one-on-one games in the family driveway?

"No, because there's an eleven-year age gap between us," he said. When Anthony left home to play for Bradley University, Candace was going into the second grade. She was still in elementary school when Anthony was a rookie with the Philadelphia 76ers.

One day Candace, who was a standout soccer and basketball player, asked her mother, "How can I live up to Anthony and Marcus? Anthony is this great basketball player, and Marcus is studying to become a doctor."

Sara smiled. "Don't worry. You can do anything you want—become a basketball player or become a doctor."

Candace chose basketball, and the rest is history.

The only brother-sister combination that compares to Team Parker is Reggie and Cheryl Miller. Some say Cheryl is the best woman basketball player of all time, and Reggie was no slouch, either, playing in some memorable games with the Indiana Pacers during his storied eighteen-year pro career. Today, he works as an NBA commentator on TNT.

Which begs an intriguing question: since Anthony and Candace are ten to twenty years younger than Reggie and Cheryl Miller, how many baskets would they have to spot them in a two-on-two match up?

FILLING A VOID

Away from home for the first time, Anthony went through a time of transition during his freshman year of college. His coach at Bradley, Jim Molinari, was a Christian, and he'd invite the team chaplain to share a devotional thought after pregame meals. Players could stay and attend, or they were free to leave. The chaplain program was part of a Campus Crusade for Christ ministry.

Anthony was intrigued enough to stick around to listen to the chaplain. He hadn't gone to church much growing up . . . his parents were Christmas-and-Easter churchgoers, so his exposure to the Gospel was limited. But Anthony felt a void in his heart, like something was missing in his life.

Sure, he was a good person who came from a good family. Sure, he had never been a problem to his parents or gone through a rebellious stage. Sure, he was respectful to his coaches and showed a willingness to work hard on the basketball floor as well as on his academic studies. The adults in his life called him a model kid.

But Anthony knew in his heart that he wasn't perfect—and that only one person who ever lived fit that description: Jesus Christ.

Anthony continued to attend team chapels and developed

a friendship with the chaplain, Dick Belsley, who invited him to drop by his office so they could talk about questions he had about Christianity. They had long discussions about how God desired to have a personal relationship with Anthony, and about how believing and accepting the truth of the death and resurrection of Jesus Christ was the only way he could enter into a personal relationship with the Lord of the universe and begin his walk with God.

Eventually Anthony said yes to Jesus Christ. He didn't understand a lot about what it meant to be a Christian, but if the Lord was willing to meet him where he was, then Anthony was willing to take His hand.

Meanwhile, Anthony excelled on and off the basketball court at Bradley. While fashioning a fine four-year playing career at Bradley, which is part of the Missouri Valley Conference, he majored in chemistry his first three years before switching to liberal arts and sciences his senior year. Anthony was never an All-American player or even talked about much outside the conference, but he had an explosive first step, slashed well to the hoop, and was an efficient shooter with great mechanics. His best year was his junior season, when he averaged nearly 19 points a game and was named the Missouri Valley Conference MVP.

Even though Anthony was an excellent player, he played in a "mid-major" conference that didn't send a lot of players to the NBA. Several NBA scouts, however, saw something special in him. They liked the unselfish way he played the game, how he exhibited good court vision, and how he made everyone around him play better.

Even though he was well regarded, the Bradley product

still raised a few eyebrows when the New Jersey Nets selected him with the twenty-first pick in the 1997 NBA draft. The Nets promptly traded him to the Philadelphia 76ers in a multiplayer deal. (Does this story sound familiar? That's exactly what happened to Kyle Korver, who also played for a Missouri Valley school—Creighton University—and was also drafted by the Nets, who immediately traded him to Philly.)

Although Anthony was regarded highly enough to be a first-round draft pick, he wasn't regarded highly enough to play much his first year in the NBA. He was typecast as a tenth or eleventh man who came off the bench for a few spot minutes or who got in late in the game when the outcome was decided (that's called "garbage time" in the NBA).

Anthony languished on the 76ers bench throughout his rookie season, appearing in only thirty-nine regular season contests and averaging just five minutes a game. But then again, the guy playing ahead of him—a fellow named Allen Iverson—had a way of not only sucking up all the oxygen in the room but also of taking all the playing time.

Iverson, whose cornrows, tattoos, arm sleeves, and headband represented the hip-hop culture in the NBA, was the same age as Anthony but was already in his fourth season in the league when Anthony arrived. He had turned pro after his freshmen year—called a "one and done"—at Georgetown University and become an NBA star overnight. Despite his diminutive size (he stands only 6 feet tall), the blazing-quick point guard scored at will and ran the show in Philadelphia.

In Philly, Allen Iverson was known as "The Answer." Anthony, on the other hand, was "The Question," as in "Would he catch on with the team?"

The answer: not for long.

Injuries and the fact that he didn't fit into the offensive scheme with Iverson around conspired against him. At 6 foot, 6 inches tall and weighing 215 pounds, Anthony had the prototypical size for an NBA shooting guard. He was a good scorer from the perimeter, which can accompany any threats the team may have had inside the paint. The scouting report on him was that he was not an elite run-and-jump athlete like Iverson, although he could be deceptively quick and very fluid with the ball in his hands. On the defensive side of the ball, he made some plays but was not known for having a lot of lateral quickness.

Ankle injuries kept Anthony on the bench during his first two seasons in the league, and at one point he was put on the injured reserve list with a broken foot. With one year left on his three-year rookie contract, Philadelphia shipped him off to the Orlando Magic, where he also didn't last long, playing in only sixteen games. The Magic waived him—meaning he was released—and no other NBA team picked him up.

Needing a basketball job—and to gain some confidence—Anthony dropped down to the minor league Continental Basketball Association (CBA) and finished the season with the Quad City Thunder in Iowa. He hoped a strong summer league showing with the Toronto Raptors would fast-track him back into the NBA, but he got hurt again, which doused any hopes of landing with another NBA team anytime soon.

If Anthony was going to resurrect his career, he would have to play overseas.

THE ROAD TO ISRAEL

Anthony's agent shopped him around to various teams in Europe and Asia. The most interest came from Maccabi Tel Aviv, who said they'd take a flier on him.

"Maccabi Tel Aviv was really the only team I considered," Anthony said. "For me, it just felt like this is where the Lord was telling me to go. Maccabi was a high-level team coming off a strong season, losing the final of the Euroleague championships, so it was a great situation for me. As an American playing basketball, Israel is one of the best countries I could go to because a lot of people speak English and a lot of Americans live there. But I didn't know that before I agreed to come."

Just like that, Anthony Parker, who had never been outside North America, was moving to Israel with his wife of one year, Tamy. Talk about a major adjustment. Whereas Anthony's first three years of professional basketball could be likened to the Hebrews wandering in the wilderness—meaning he wasn't getting anywhere—now he was confident God had set a path for him. Since that path was taking him and his wife to Israel, they followed that course in faith. Little did he know that saying yes to Maccabi Tel Aviv would lead to a five-year stint in the *real* Promised Land and pave the way back to the NBA.

Maccabi Tel Aviv, Israel's top professional basketball team, usually qualified to play in the Euroleague, which is the highest level and most important professional basketball competition in Europe. Teams from up to eighteen different countries compete. (Geographically, Israel is actually part of Asia but is a member of FIBA Europe, the federation that governs European basketball.)

European basketball is a lot like Premier League soccer in Europe in that a team must beat out regional and national competition to qualify for the Euroleague. Twenty-four teams qualify for Euroleague competition, which starts every fall with games eventually feeding into playoff rounds, just like in the NBA. A "Final Four" tournament, featuring the winners of four quarterfinal series, play each other in one-off knockout games held at a predetermined site. The semifinal winners vie for the European championship; the semifinal losers play for third place.

Maccabi Tel Aviv, originally founded in 1906 as the Maccabi Tel Aviv Sports Club, was the biggest and most successful sports team in Israel. It's hard to explain to Americans how big a deal Maccabi is in Israel, but try to think of the Boston Celtics, New York Yankees, and Pittsburgh Steelers all rolled into one. Maccabi plays in the modern Nokia Arena, which is located in the Yad Eliyahu area of Tel Aviv—Israel's capital city.

Maccabi plays a brand of basketball that's just a notch under the level played in the NBA. For more than twenty-five years, NBA teams have either traveled to Europe or invited Euroleague teams to come to the United States for a series of preseason games. The NBA teams win more than nine times out of ten, but these exhibition contests are close and hard-fought. The Euro teams have some very talented players, and when they step on a basketball court with an NBA team, they play as if they have something to prove.

The gap between the NBA and Euroleague teams is narrowing, although it must be noted that Europe's best players are now playing in the NBA. In the past two years, Euroleague has changed its rules to make them more like the rules in the NBA. For example, the Euroleague altered the size of its three-second key, also known as the "paint." The awkward trapezoid lane was changed to a good old-fashioned rectangle, and the three-point line was extended to almost match the NBA's.

Historically, Maccabi had shown Yankees-like dominance of Israeli basketball by winning every Israeli League title since 1970, except in 1992–93. Seen around the world as the face of Jewish sport, the team was held in high esteem as Israel's national sporting representative. With a sizable budget to sign players, Maccabi's team usually included four to six Israelis, a couple of Americans, and a pair of dual-nationality players like Derrick Sharp and David Sternlight, who were Americans with Israeli citizenship because of marriage or ancestry.

This was the situation Anthony was getting into when he agreed to play for Maccabi and move to Israel—and the first few weeks in Tel Aviv were an eye-opener for him.

Anthony and Tamy had no sooner landed and moved into their apartment when an event called the "Second Intifada"—or uprising—broke out on September 28, 2000. The conflict started after Israel's then-opposition leader, Ariel Sharon, visited the Temple Mount in Jerusalem. Since the site was sacred to both the Islamic and Jewish religions, the question of sovereignty remained a thorny issue between Israel and the Palestinians.

To protest their displeasure at Sharon's visit to the Temple Mount, Palestinian demonstrators threw stones at Jewish worshippers at the Wailing Wall, which prompted Israeli security forces to fire rubber-coated metal bullets and live ammunition at the crowd. Five Palestinians were killed, setting off another vicious cycle of violence.

Violence escalated rapidly, going from rock throwing to machine gun and mortar fire to suicide bombings and lethal road ambushes. Over the next five years of insurrection, Palestinians killed more than a thousand Israelis, and Israeli security forces killed nearly five thousand Palestinians in retaliatory raids.

This was the backdrop as Anthony joined the biggest symbol of Israeli sport—the Maccabi Tel Aviv basketball team.

"It was tough," Anthony said, putting it mildly. "This was the first time I left my country, and suddenly there was a war forty-five minutes from my doorsteps. CNN was covering it in a big way. My family back in the States watched what was happening in the Middle East, so they were calling me and wanting me to come home. Tamy was hearing the same from her family. Initially, we stayed in our apartment as much as we could, but then we started venturing out. When I went out into the streets, I saw that life was normal. I saw kids going to school and people shopping in malls. The buses were running and restaurants were open. Everything was normal, or what passes for 'normal' in the Middle East."

Part of that "normal" was the way security became a second way of life. Any time Anthony or his wife went out in Israel, they had to be prepared to open her purse or backpack before entering any public building or even private establishments. "Everywhere you go in public, the security forces can and will open your purse or wand you," Anthony said. "If you are driving into an underground parking lot, they will look in your backseat and make you open your car trunk."

Security was especially intense around the Maccabi basketball team, which was a target-rich environment since the
team was a national treasure. "We always had beefed-up security with Maccabi," he said. "We'd have armed men with
us at the hotels and on the bus. We had police escorts everywhere we went. For us, that was all part of playing basketball
for an Israeli team."

Even games played *outside* Israel reminded Anthony that
he could never really escape what was happening back in the
Middle East. Energized fans in European cities like Paris,
Rome, and Berlin waved Palestinian flags and chanted emotional slogans Anthony couldn't understand. Some rallying
calls he *could* understand, like the fans in Barcelona who
chanted, "Boycott Israel, Viva Palestine."

How did he cope?

By doing what his Israeli teammates had learned to do
long ago: he got used to it.

"I lived in a culture of people who had developed a thick
skin to what was going on around them," he explained.
"When we first moved there, a bomb would go off in Jerusalem or one of the cities nearby and kill some people. Tamy
and I would say, 'Whoa! They're killing people out there!' But
my teammates and coaches would tell us, 'Don't worry about
it. It's thirty minutes away.' Slowly but surely, we got desensi-
tized to the violence happening around us."

Fans attending games at the Nokia Arena had to pass
through airport-like screening, including stepping through
metal detectors and being subjected to searches. What authorities *did* allow into the basketball arena surprised Anthony. "Fans could bring in flares and horns, which they

don't allow in the States," he said. "They could also bring in flags, drums, and trumpets, just like they could for soccer games. So fans over there were very passionate and used to making a lot of noise.

"But as I like to tell people, I felt safer in Tel Aviv than in most cities back in the U.S. It seems like the Israelis are in a perpetual state of war, and often in times of war, the crimes inside that country go down. There's just so much nationalistic pride that you don't have a whole lot of rape cases and murders and things like that. Sure, you can be in a situation where you are in the wrong place at the wrong time, but overall, I felt safe when I lived in Israel. I did not feel like my life was in danger from anyone around me."

One thing Anthony and his wife refused to do, however, was ride a bus—a popular target of suicide bombers willing to unleash their murderous mayhem. And he learned to keep his eyes open his first year in Tel Aviv, something that becomes second nature to anyone living in that region of the world.

And then the events of September 11 took place, and Anthony and Tamy were far from home. They clung to each other and got through it. "What I remember is how supportive the world was of America after 9/11," he said. "I talked to friends and people I knew in Israel, and everybody took it the same way as Americans did. For a time, it seemed that the world was united against such a horrific terrorist attack, but unfortunately, that did not last."

Not long after the Twin Towers went down, Palestinians set off a weeklong wave of bombings in and around Jerusalem and Tel Aviv. "That was the closest we came to leaving," Anthony said. "My wife was pregnant at the time, and the medical facility where she got her ultrasounds done was around the corner from a bombing attack, so that was close.

"But we were forming relationships with people and the community, and we felt like we just couldn't leave them. We used to do things as a team where we would go to the hospitals and see kids and families who had gotten injured by mortar or missile attacks. It's a lot different when you meet these people in person. It used to be that I would see footage on CNN and hear the announcer say, 'Five people killed and ten injured,' and I didn't know what that really meant until I went into those hospitals and saw how these attacks affected families and their lives."

Anthony and Tamy became good friends with a family whose daughter had paid a heavy price just for being in the wrong place at the wrong time. She was hanging out with some friends in a pizza restaurant when a young Palestinian male walked in with a backpack, which he placed on the table. Then he announced to everyone in the restaurant, "See you on the other side." He detonated the explosives in the backpack, which was also filled with nails and screws. The suicide bomber died instantly, believing he would be rewarded for killing "infidels."

Several people were killed in the attack, but Anthony's friends' daughter somehow survived. "This girl had a whole lot of complications as a result of that suicide mission," Anthony said. "Developing a relationship with the family and seeing how their lives were affected by that physically and psychologically gave me a whole different perspective on these kinds of events happening around the world."

RETRACING JESUS' STEPS

The violence and threats of violence were the downside of living in Israel during a tumultuous time in history that continues today. But there was an upside for Anthony, and that was a once-in-a-lifetime opportunity to live in the Holy Land.

Anthony was staying in the land God gave His chosen people, the Israelites, after He delivered them from slavery under the Pharaoh of Egypt. This was Canaan, the land of milk and honey that was also known as the "Promised Land." Jerusalem became the political and spiritual center of the ancient Jewish kingdom, the city where David reigned and where his son, Solomon, constructed the Temple. A small portion of the historical Temple, the Western Wall—also known as the Wailing Wall—still stands in a part of Jerusalem called the Temple Mount, which, as Anthony quickly learned after his arrival in Tel Aviv, was perhaps the most hotly contested area in the Holy Land.

"My faith grew so much, going to Israel and being a Christian," Anthony said. "I saw places that I read about in the Old Testament. I took a couple of tours, like to the Jordan River and the Sea of Galilee, where Jesus walked on water. I saw a lot of the country during my five years there, but there were areas that were off-limits, like the West Bank. But I went to the Negev in the south, the wilderness area where the Hebrews wandered for forty years. Just seeing all this history and being part of it grew my faith. I also observed a lot of the traditions that were talked about in the Old Testament that the Israelis still observe today," he said.

"Being a Christian and reading the Bible and being able to see the different cities and different landmarks discussed in the

Bible was amazing. My time there was something I wish everyone could experience. I couldn't put a price tag on it."

Over the next few years, Anthony's friends and family would come to Israel to visit him and his wife. They would arrive in Israel at Tel Aviv's Ben Gurion International Airport with one mind-set and then depart with a whole new way of looking at the nation. "I just wish more people would go over there and experience the things I did," he said.

Even though ambling through streets Jesus and the apostles likely walked on nearly two thousand years ago was awe-inspiring as well as inspirational to Anthony's faith, he knew that he was being paid a lot of shekels to play basketball for Maccabi—and the team expected a good return on its investment.

You could say Maccabi invested wisely.

Anthony had an unbelievable five-year career with Maccabi, plus two short stints with an Italian team, Pallacanestro Virtus Roma. In fact, he went from being a forgotten man in the NBA to someone the league scouting website Draftexpress.com called "hands down the best player in the world outside of the NBA."

So how did that happen?

After settling into Tel Aviv during the Second Intifada, Anthony—by now healed of his injuries—knew he would have to make some adjustments in his game. Sure, the fundamentals of European basketball were the same as those in the NBA: pass, dribble, shoot, defend, rebound, screen, play hard, and play together. But there were important differences, starting with the basketball court, which was three feet shorter from end to end with a trapezoid-shaped lane that was wider on the baseline but narrower at the free throw line. This meant post players tended to set up position higher in the lane, which impacted the offensive flow. Americans playing the guard position, like Anthony, often felt like there was nowhere to drive toward the basket.

In addition, there was no defensive three-second rule in European basketball (in the NBA, players aren't allowed to stand in the lane without guarding someone for more than three seconds), which clogged the lane and also reduced spacing between players. Also, the three-point line in European basketball was nearly two feet closer than it is in the NBA, which meant shooters were *looking* for the three-point opportunity and expected to launch—and make—plenty of three-point shots.

Another important difference was that European games were forty minutes long, matching the length of American college games but shorter than the NBA's forty-eight minutes. A shorter game impacted substitutions, rotations, and effort levels since players didn't have to pace themselves as much as they did in the NBA.

And then there was the officiating. In European basketball, it's not uncommon to have three officials from three different countries—all with different interpretations on what constituted traveling, a foul, or a legal screen. European officials, he discovered, loved to call offensive charges, so there was a lot of "flopping" by 7-foot centers when much-smaller point guards bumped into them on drives to the basket.

But the biggest difference, Anthony found, was the team aspect that permeated the culture of European basketball. Teams didn't "clear out" one side of the court to let their best player—their Kobe or LeBron—go one-on-one. There was more willingness to involve everyone in the offense and pass the ball around.

Anthony learned that the "extra pass" was the norm rather than the exception in the European game. Case in point: penetrating the lane with the dribble is a big part of the international and NBA game, but a European player usually looks to pass rather than score—unless he has a clear lay-in.

"The way the rules are in the NBA, you can be more one-on-one and get to the basket, and teams put a premium on that in the U.S.," Anthony explained, "while in Europe, you're almost forced by the rules to move the ball around and play in more of a team setting."

Though European teams don't play as many games—usually between sixty and seventy per season—as NBA clubs, it's still a long season that starts with training camp in August and ends in late May with the Euroleague championships. With fewer games on the schedule, Anthony and his teammates practiced more, which turned out to be to his benefit because it helped him to improve his game while he was in Europe.

Maccabi had signed Anthony to fill a void at shooting guard left by Doron Sheffer's retirement. Sheffer, an Israeli who grew up in a kibbutz, had played guard for the University of Connecticut back in the mid-1990s. He was good enough that the Los Angeles Clippers drafted him in the second round of the 1996 NBA draft, but he chose to sign with Maccabi. After four productive seasons, however, the twenty-eight-year-old Israeli was staggered to learn that he had cancer. He retired suddenly to undergo treatments and to travel around the world to places like India, South America, and Costa Rica, where he could escape the public eye.

News of Sheffer's cancer and travels dominated coverage on Israeli sports pages, and Anthony can be excused for feeling like Babe Dahlgren, the first baseman who replaced ailing New York Yankee Lou Gehrig in 1939. Sheffer was held up as one of Israel's greatest basketball players, and now Anthony was being called in to pick up the slack while Sheffer fought a cancerous tumor.

Anthony did more than that—he grabbed the reins of leadership on Maccabi by becoming both a scorer and a playmaker for the team during his "rookie" season, when he helped the Tel Aviv team win its first Euroleague championship in *twenty* years. He had a captivating style of play that made it impossible for fans to take their eyes off of him. The Israeli fans, ecstatic to be cheering a winner again, accepted him as one of their own.

Anthony loved playing in Israel, and although Maccabi didn't repeat as European champions in 2001–02, he had firmly established himself as a fan favorite. But then Tamy became pregnant, and that complicated matters. As the birth of Tamy's first child approached, and as certain hormones began kicking in, she understandably began feeling the need to be back home in the United States. Anthony comprehended his wife's desire to be near hearth and family, so he agreed to take a six-month sabbatical from the game, meaning he wouldn't be returning to Maccabi for the start of his third season with the team.

Anthony and Tamy returned to Florida, where she gave birth in late 2002 to a son they named Alonso. Once mother and son were feeling settled, Anthony needed to get back to work. He took a short gig with a prominent Italian team,

Pallacanestro Virtus Roma, and played the last half of the 2002–03 season in Rome.

Anthony could have stayed in Italy, but all along he wanted to return to Israel, a country he and Tamy had grown to love. Maccabi wanted him back, and so did the Israeli fans, who held high hopes for the coming season. Maccabi had lured former head coach Pini Gershon out of a two-year retirement because there was a strong feeling that the team had the horses to go back to the Final Four and win the Euroleague championship—which would be played in Tel Aviv!

So imagine the excitement among Israeli fans when Maccabi won the Israeli domestic championship and the Israeli National Cup to qualify for the Euroleague playoffs. But once again—as in 2000 with the Second Intifada and 9/11—the real world intruded onto the playing court. Not only was the Second Intifada still in the news (a truce wouldn't be called until 2005), but President George W. Bush commenced Operation Iraqi Freedom on March 20, 2003. Many Israelis feared that Saddam Hussein would retaliate by firing Scud missiles toward Israel's major cities—a tactic he used in the first Gulf War, when he launched forty-seven Scuds toward Israel.

Would Saddam launch missiles toward Israel again?

The answer was no, but that didn't mean that the Israeli populace wasn't unconcerned or unprepared. Israel had an impressive civil defense system in place. Since 1951, all Israeli homes, residential buildings, and industrial buildings were required to have bomb shelters, which people were supposed to enter after hearing a warning siren. Anthony and Tamy even had gas masks at the ready, but the attacks from Iraq never materialized.

The Euroleague Final Four, scheduled for late April in Tel Aviv, nearly didn't come off because of Israel's support of the United States. This led to a huge controversy, and other Euroleague teams tried to move the Euroleague Final Four out of Tel Aviv. But in the end, the Final Four stayed in Israel, and Maccabi gave the citizenry something to cheer about during another time of apprehension and uncertainty. Even better, the home team lifted the country's spirits by defeating CSKA Moscow in the semifinals and then annihilating Skipper Bologna 118–74 in the finals to win the Euroleague championship.

Anthony was named as the Final Four MVP, which only further cemented his status as a sports hero in Israel. The following season (2004–05), Anthony and his teammates backed up their Euroleague championship by winning it again. That season, the Final Four was played in Moscow, and Maccabi Tel Aviv defeated TAU Cerámica, a Spanish team, in the final. Anthony wasn't named as the Final Four MVP this time, but he walked away with something better—the Euroleague Most Valuable Player trophy.

Anthony was now a big deal in Israel, and his handsome face graced billboards around Tel Aviv with advertisements for Nissan Pathfinders. He was also featured in the TV ad campaign for the car.

Some commentators believed Anthony was the most complete swingman (a player who can play guard or forward) in the history of European basketball. The way his game blossomed since he first traveled overseas to play astounded the basketball experts. They all agreed that he was not the same the player he was when he joined Maccabi back in 2000.

THE JUMP SHOT THAT BROUGHT
ANTHONY PARKER HOME

The first exhibition game between an NBA team and a European team was played in 1978 between the Washington Bullets and Maccabi Tel Aviv. The Bullets (renamed the Wizards in 1997) were the defending NBA champions when they traveled to Israel for this historic game. They probably wished they hadn't boarded the charter jet: the Washington Bullets lost in a shocker, 98–97.

It would be another six years before another NBA team ventured to Europe. In August of 1984, the New Jersey Nets and the Phoenix Suns journeyed to Yad Eliyahu Arena in Tel Aviv. Both teams lost to Maccabi on consecutive nights.

Maccabi played six more exhibitions against NBA teams over the next twenty years but lost them all. After Maccabi Tel Aviv won back-to-back European championships in 2004 and 2005, though, the basketball world took notice. The Maccabi team was invited to play the Toronto Raptors in a preseason game in Toronto. For the first time in five years, Anthony would play against NBA competition.

For Anthony and his Maccabi teammates, this was Game 7 of the NBA Finals. Just days before the start of the 2005–06 NBA season, a sellout crowd of 17,281 fans filled Air Canada Centre for the mid-October game. NBA commissioner David Stern was there, along with the consular general for Israel in Toronto and a huge contingent of Jewish fans eager to see their sports heroes.

They were treated to quite a game. The game was tied 103–103 with 11 seconds left. Maccabi had the ball, and after a timeout the ball was put into Anthony's hands. This time, his teammates uncharacteristically cleared out the right side of the court for Anthony, who was isolated with Morris Peterson guarding him. He made a move on Peterson and then pulled up for a twenty-footer that swished the net with .8 second on the clock.

After Toronto's desperation three-point attempt at the final buzzer missed, giving Maccabi the win, Anthony's clutch jumper was the talk of the basketball world. This was the first time since 1988 that an NBA team had lost a sanctioned international game and only the second such defeat in the past twenty-eight games. Anthony's winning jumper impressed the Toronto Raptors coaching staff, who filed that information away. The following July, when the Raptors were in the midst of overhauling the team, they asked Anthony to come back to the NBA after a six-year hiatus.

Anthony didn't have to be asked twice. He signed with the Raptors and quickly established himself as the team's starting shooting guard and as a player who could handle the three-point shooting duties. He finished fourth in the NBA in three-point shooting during his first season back and was credited with helping the Raptors clinch their first-ever division title in the 2006–07 season and their first NBA playoff berth in five years.

Anthony was in his early thirties, and he was making the most of his second chance in the NBA. He played three seasons with Toronto before signing a two-year deal with the LeBron James–led Cleveland Cavaliers in 2009.

Before the 2010–11 season, however, LeBron left the Cavaliers after a much-ballyhooed signing with Miami that allowed him to join Dwyane Wade and Chris Bosh with the

Heat. Without the player many considered the best in the NBA to lead them, the Cavaliers floundered in the 2010–11 season, winning just 19 games and losing 63. The Cavs' lowlight that season was when they set a dubious NBA record by losing twenty-six games in a row.

Anthony's contract with the Cleveland Cavaliers expired at the end of the 2010–11 season. With Cleveland doing some housecleaning during the season, coupled with the expiration of the NBA's collective bargaining agreement during the summer of 2011 and a possible lockout or shortened season in 2011–12, Anthony is not sure when or where he'll play next.

Who knows?

Maybe the Lord is calling him back to Israel—to Maccabi Tel Aviv.

4

CHRIS KAMAN:
GETTING OFF THE MEDS

"Did you take your pill this morning?"

Chris Kaman says he heard that question about ten times a day from the adults in his life while growing up in the Grand Rapids, Michigan area. What his parents, schoolteachers, school nurses, and administrators were *really* asking was this: *Did you take your Ritalin with breakfast?*

They had good reason to ask.

Chris had been a little monster since his toddler days, when his parents, Leroy and Pam, began wondering what to do with the whirling dervish of misbehavior on their hands. Their rambunctious son would do anything or say anything that came to mind. One time, he whacked his sleeping father with an Etch A Sketch, bloodying his nose. He threw toys against walls and kicked over Lego creations. He was always testing boundaries and coming up with creative ways to cause trouble, sending Pam to the local library to read all the books she could about raising children.

"I'd tell him to brush his teeth, and he'd put up a fight," Pam said. "I'd tell him to put on his pajamas, and we'd fight. Go to bed, and another fight. I tell people that it was much worse than anybody could have dreamed of. We couldn't go to an amusement park or to a movie together. He couldn't stay still. He couldn't concentrate. He was all over the place."

Pam ultimately became so exasperated at Chris' antics that after church one day she tearfully confessed to her pastor, M. Wayne Benson, that she wanted to give Chris away to someone who could do a better job raising him. She loved Chris dearly, but her young son was driving her crazy.

Pastor Benson comforted Pam. "Just be patient," he said. "You won't always feel this way. Things will get better."

Meanwhile, four or five babysitters quit on Pam because they had grown so exasperated trying to handle Chris. The babysitters who didn't quit had to be ready for anything.

One high school girl, Amy Farrell, was asked to look after Chris, then two-and-a-half, and his older brother Michael (who was seven years old) while the parents attended a wedding rehearsal and dinner for Chris' Aunt Carole.

Just before dark, Michael bounded down the steps to the backyard to feed Shadow, the Kamans' black Labrador puppy. When Michael had trouble freeing Shadow from a chain around his neck, he called out for help. Amy stepped outside to assist Michael, then looked back just in time to see Chris slam the back door shut, which automatically locked the door. She and Michael immediately shouted for Chris to open up, but he refused.

Christopher Zane Kaman, not yet three years old, was ruler of the house now. Ignoring the loud banging on the door, he set a chair next to the stove and put a frying pan atop one of the burners. Then he poured some Pringles potato chips into the pan and squeezed ketchup over the chips. He wanted to do some cooking, and what better way than to prepare a snack out of two of his favorite foods?

A boy in his terrible twos, a hot stove, and no parents around . . . this was getting serious. Michael ran to a nearby neighbor for help. Together, they found an open window and took the screen off to gain access back into the home—and save everyone from disaster.

Stuff like that happened all the time during Chris' childhood, but don't get the idea that Chris was born to permissive parents who lost control of a son they doted on. His father and mother were traditional, God-fearing parents who believed that sparing the rod would spoil the child. They were on board with Dr. Dobson's *Dare to Discipline* and attempted to instill godly values by the seat of the pants—meaning they weren't averse to giving Chris a couple of good whacks on his bottom when his behavior warranted it.

They were also salt-of-the-earth parents: Leroy was a city employee for Wyoming, a suburb of Grand Rapids. He plowed streets, fixed potholes and water main breaks, and painted fire hydrants, while Pam worked in the Wyoming Police Department, senior citizen center, and the accounting office for the municipality.

Larry and Pam wanted to raise their children in the admonition of the Lord, and if they could get Chris to sit still long enough, they read him books with Bible lessons and took him to church on Sundays.

When Chris started school and his younger sister Jessica came along, Pam quit working for the city and ran a day care out of her home. She also cleaned houses to help cover tuition at Tri-Unity Christian School because she and her husband believed strongly in Christian education. *Whatever it takes to keep them in a Christian school* was their motto.

Even though Pam and Leroy spanked Chris, put him in "time-outs," and regularly scolded him for his willful misbehavior, nothing worked during those early childhood years. Even before the locking-out-the-babysitter incident, Pam came to believe that the situation was serious enough to talk to her family doctor about Chris' behavior. But the doctor just patted Pam on the shoulder and told her Chris was just going through a phase and would turn out just fine. "He'll grow out of it," he said.

Except that he didn't. In fact, as he grew older, his behavior became more unruly than ever. They visited a new family doctor, Dr. Janet Talmo, and she referred them to the Ken-O-Sha Diagnostic Center in Grand Rapids, which offered testing for off-the-wall kids like Chris. For half a day, Ken-O-Sha evaluators watched from behind a one-way mirror as Chris, then around two-and-a-half, played with puzzles and interacted with other kids.

A week later, Leroy and Pam received the bad news: their son had been diagnosed with Attention-Deficit Hyperactivity Disorder, or ADHD. The recommendation: give the boy the antihistamine Benadryl (for sedation purposes) and enroll him in a Pre-Primary Impaired program (PPI) at Eastern Elementary School, which was part of the Grand Rapids Public School system.

The Ken-O-Sha evaluators told Pam her son wouldn't be ready for kindergarten until he attended the PPI pre-kindergarten program to work out his behavioral kinks. That meant having Chris board a yellow school bus—the "short bus" for handicapped or special-needs children—each morning so he could be transported across Grand Rapids.

It wasn't Chris' fault that he had to take the little yellow bus. In those pre-kindergarten days, he could no more sit still or take an afternoon nap on the classroom carpet than he could dunk a basketball.

Whenever he got into trouble at the PPI school—which seemed to happen every five minutes—his teacher would tell him, "Time to go in the barrel." In Chris' classroom was a wooden barrel lying on its side that had enough room inside for a misbehaving student to crawl into for a short period of "time-out." After several minutes inside the barrel, Chris would rejoin the class, but it wasn't long before he'd forget about the punishment and start throwing plush toys at the other kids or taking off his belt and swinging it above his head. Then it was another crawl into the wooden barrel for yet another cooling-off period.

Even as a preschooler, Chris was big for his age, so he looked a lot older. Shortly after starting the PPI program, the teacher asked Chris if he knew his birthday.

"Apprul twenty-eight," he replied.

"How old are you?"

Chris held up two fingers.

"No, you're three years old," corrected the teacher.

Chris wouldn't back down. "I'm two!" he said, holding up two fingers.

No wonder the teacher thought Chris should be further down the maturity road—because of his size, she was convinced he was a year older than he really was!

When Chris was about three-and-a-half years old, the PPI administrators strongly recommended that he be put on Ritalin, a potent anti-depressant, to manage his ADHD.

Leroy and Pam figured the school authorities knew what was best and agreed to give the drug a try.

"We trusted the professionals and put Chris on Ritalin," Pam said. "They also told us he would eventually grow out of it. I remember one doctor saying, 'You don't see adults bouncing off a couch.' At the same time, though, Chris' ADHD diagnosis was based on a few forms filled out by a couple of teachers back during the half day of testing at Ken-O-Sha Diagnostic Center. The school psychologist reviewed them in a matter of minutes and made a judgment that would impact Chris for the rest of his life."

When Chris reached elementary school age, Leroy and Pam enrolled him in Tri-Unity Christian School, which was about a half hour from their home. Even though Christ took Ritalin during the school day—he didn't have to take his "medicine" during the weekends—he was still a handful during his early elementary school years.

Chris didn't misbehave just at school either. He'd take other kids' bikes and dump them on the railroad tracks or climb on neighborhood roofs—just for the heck of it. One time, Pam was sitting on her front porch, visiting with her sister-in-law, when she looked up at the neighbor's house across the street. There was Chris, eight years old, moving around on the roof. She got up, feeling her heart in her throat, and calmly walked across the street. She didn't want to yell at him and cause him to make a fast move—and slip off the roof.

Chris wasn't mean-spirited toward other children or a bully—just out-of-control and goofy. He was also very impressionable. His older brother Michael said he and other kids in the neighborhood often dared Chris to do crazy stunts. He was too immature to say no.

You're daring me? Then watch this . . .

Chris' rowdy behavior even when he was on Ritalin prompted head scratching from his parents as well as his doctor. Ritalin was supposed to mellow him out—make him docile and obedient—but that wasn't happening. That's why people at school often asked him whether he had taken his medication that morning.

"I hated being asked all the time to take a pill to make myself regular," he said. "That drove me just as crazy."

Chris was always scheduled to take his second pill of the day in the nurse's office during morning recess. The school nurse would hand him a pill and a glass of water. The ritual was repeated in the afternoon, too.

Chris didn't know it at the time, and neither did his parents, but he was a pawn in a system where health care professionals, school administrators, and teachers make snap judgments about boys who have continual ants in their pants. (Boys get tagged with attention-deficit disorder three to six times as often as girls.) Once a child has been diagnosed with ADHD, doctors and psychologists hand the parents a prescription for Ritalin . . . and that's when the ADHD train leaves the station.

The Drug Enforcement Agency has classified Ritalin as

a Schedule II drug—a designation reserved for the most addictive and dangerous drugs that can be legally prescribed. For nearly fifteen years, Chris took Ritalin or another antidepressant called Adderall. He was among the six million kids under the age of eighteen who take these drugs daily. Some of these kids are given these drugs as freely as kids who are given Flintstone Chewable Vitamins to start their day.

Ritalin's side effects include decreased appetite, trouble sleeping, headache, irritability, stomachache, mood swings, and nausea—and Chris experienced them all. Ritalin's main side effect on Chris was to depress his appetite, but it didn't make him any easier to manage. For most of his early school years, Chris was forced to sit next to his teacher lest he disrupt the class again.

GROWING LIKE A BEANPOLE

Looking back, Chris knew he was a handful for his teachers and for his parents.

"My dad is very old school and traditional," he said. "His father was in the military, and he served in the military. When I'd done something wrong, I got either the belt or the paddle from him, but it was usually this handball paddle with a person's face on it. My brother and I called him 'Harry.' So when I heard Dad or Mom say, 'Go get the paddle,' that meant doing the dreaded paddle walk. Then I'd get one or two good whacks from Harry."

Chris also received spankings at Tri-Unity Christian School. At the beginning of the school year, the Tri-Unity principal would send letters to the parents asking for permission to spank their children under certain circumstances—

and with witnesses present for everyone's protection. Up until the sixth grade, Chris heard his teachers utter the dreaded command several times a year: *That's enough, young man. Go report to the principal's office.*

"Whenever I got sent to the principal's office, I'd walk in where the principal and another teacher would be waiting for me. Then I'd have to put my hands on the principal's desk, and she would say, 'Butt out.' Then she'd give me a couple of good whacks. Early on I cried, but as I got older, say around the fifth grade, I had trouble keeping a straight face. One time I laughed, which got me into more trouble. I was suspended for that episode."

The parent-approved spankings eventually stopped in middle school, but the attempts to keep Chris in check continued. Poor classroom behavior resulted in "early birds"—going to school before first period and writing lines in a notebook—or losing rights and privileges at home. He was often grounded from playing with friends, playing video games, or enjoying other fun activities.

There were times, though, when Chris would surprise his parents by coming home with a gold-colored "Godly Character" award his teacher had given him after he had done something noteworthy in class. One time, his teacher praised him by writing, "Chris was such a good helper today. He helped me clean out my marker drawer." Another time, Chris found money on the playground and gave it to his teacher so she could find the rightful owner. The amount: eleven cents. The money was later taped to a "Godly Character" award and presented to Chris. Pam still has that award as a keepsake.

Meanwhile, Chris was growing like a beanpole and showing

impressive athletic talent on the soccer field and the basketball court. His favorite sport early on was soccer, and he was an excellent goalie, defenseman, and striker. "I liked the running part about soccer," he said. "I could run forever, and I had good footwork. My feet were pretty coordinated for a big guy."

Chris was also a good baseball player, but everyone could see he was cut out to play basketball. Tall for his age (he stood head and shoulders above his classmates), he was well coordinated, able to move well, had a deft touch as a shooter, and was very skilled around the basketball hoop.

DEALING WITH A REPUTATION

By the time Chris started high school as a freshman at Tri-Unity Christian, he had grown to 6 feet, 2 inches tall. He enjoyed athletics, but he hated everything else about school. He barely earned passing grades: his grade point average his freshman and sophomore years hovered between 1.4 and 1.6. "I did not care about schoolwork," he said. "I was at the point where I was going down and down and down."

And he was still getting into trouble for doing dumb, immature stuff in the classroom: talking out of turn, making jokes about his teachers when he thought they weren't within earshot, and flicking paper wads from his desk. At times, he felt his teachers had it out for him, based on his reputation as one of the "Ritalin kids."

"It wasn't like I was beating kids up," he said, "I wasn't doing drugs. I wasn't out there having sex. It was nothing like that. It was just dumb stuff."

What Chris and his family didn't know was that the Ritalin acted in his body like a stimulant . . . much like caffeine. In other words, the anti-ADHD pills were making him even *more* hyper.

"Basically, when a kid has ADHD, he's not paying attention. His brain is going too slow, so it's turning off a lot more than it should," Chris explained. "He has a hard time keeping attention. He doesn't focus on what he's supposed to be doing. So doctors give him a stimulant, thinking that will bring him back to normal. But in my case, I was misdiagnosed. I did *not* have ADHD, although I wouldn't discover that for a long time. But when I was taking my pills, I was basically receiving speed when I was already speeding. No wonder I was having so many behavioral problems. I was crawling out of my own skin, basically."

Chris had more and more skin to crawl out of, too. By his sophomore year, he had sprouted to 6 feet, 8 inches tall, but was as thin as a rail post at 170 pounds. During the summer before his junior year, he sprouted to 6 feet, 11 inches tall.

That same year, Chris attended a big man's basketball camp at Western Michigan University, where he played and practiced under the appraising eyes of college coaches. He must have made a strong impression at the summer camp because shortly after he got home, he received more than thirty letters from college basketball coaches expressing an interest in him playing for their teams.

But Chris knew his 1.6 grade point average would probably sink any hopes he had for playing college basketball—at least for a four-year school. So he decided to do two things:

1. Stop taking his medicine whenever he thought he could get away with it.
2. Start applying himself to his schoolwork like never before.

If his mother was watching him take his pill with break-fast, he gulped one down. But if he could fool his mom and get away without taking the pill, he'd go that route.

Chris was supposed to take his second pill of the day after third period, when students received a fifteen-minute break. He knew the drill: report to the school office, where the secretary would be waiting with his pill and cup of water. Like he did at home, when he thought he could get away with it, he'd pretend to take the Ritalin pill and then stuff it into his pants pocket. Then he'd toss the medicine into the trash can. Ditto for the afternoon pill.

Did his behavior or demeanor change?

Chris wasn't sure, but the person who knew him best at Tri-Unity was Mark Keeler, his varsity basketball coach and math teacher, and he noticed something was different about Chris—though he couldn't quite put his finger on what it was.

One day, Mr. Keeler asked Chris point-blank if he had been taking his pills.

Chris didn't want to lie, not to a coach and teacher he trusted.

"No, I haven't been taking them," he confessed.

Coach Keeler suggested a parent-teacher conference to discuss what to do. When he met with Chris' parents, they decided Chris should see a psychologist.

"When I saw this guy," Chris related, "he told me in less than ten minutes, 'You are ADHD for sure. We're going to put you on Ritalin.' But I told him I'd been on Ritalin since I was three. I hated it."

"Then let's try Adderall," replied the expert.

Adderall is a powerful stimulant that has been compared

to methamphetamine. Because of this, Adderall has a relatively high potential for abuse and addiction.

As far as Chris was concerned, it was another round of *Here we go again.*

"When I started taking Adderall at the end of my sophomore year, I tried my best to deal with it," Chris said. "Meanwhile, I knew I had to get my grades up to play college basketball, which was a great incentive. I applied myself like never before and saw a lot of improvement in my test scores and book reports. I did this through one-on-one tutoring with Coach Keeler, who really helped me. I discovered I was a hands-on learner, so if I was in a regular class where I was expected to take notes, that wasn't going to do anything for me. I'd sit in class and have five lines of notes written down after an hour, while some girl next to me would have a page and a half of notes. I just wasn't good at learning that way. But having someone sit down with me and go through the lesson material—like geometry and algebra—made all the difference."

Chris was a kinetic learner, meaning he learned best by carrying out certain physical activities. In other words, he learned by doing, which could happen when he worked one-on-one with Coach Keeler. The two other learning styles—visual learning and auditory learning, which is learning by what you see or what you hear—did not work for Chris.

Armed with a better understanding of how he learned best, Chris made rapid progress in the classroom. During his junior and senior years, he earned a 3.7 to 3.8 grade point average, which lifted his four-year average to a 2.4 or 2.6 overall—good enough to play ball at a quality four-year college.

College basketball coaches liked the fact that Chris was ambidextrous on the court, meaning he could shoot equally well with the right or left hand. Perhaps he inherited genes for this proficiency—his mom was a lefty and his father was right-handed—but don't discount the hard work he put into the game. "I was a gym rat growing up," he said. "I did the extra shooting, played pickup games all the time, but God blessed me with good hands and solid mobility."

GETTING OFF THE MEDS

Between his sophomore and junior year of high school, when Chris grew to 6 feet, 11 inches tall, he was still very thin. He couldn't gain weight, even though he drank protein shakes like they were going out of style. That was because the Ritalin and Adderall sped up his metabolism so much that everything he ate was consumed in the burning furnace of his stomach.

Another problem was what the drugs did to his appetite. When he was on his meds, Chris just wasn't very hungry. Breakfast was a bowl of cereal and a glass of juice, and lunch would be a small sandwich and an apple and chips. But watch out when dinnertime rolled around and the pills wore off. "My dinners were huge, man," he said. "My mom was a good cook who would serve us meat and potatoes Midwest style— steak, hamburgers, goulash, macaroni and cheese with tuna, lasagna, spaghetti—anything you could think of."

Despite the suppertime pig-outs, Chris could barely keep body and soul together, and he weighed just 200 pounds.

He was a standout on the high school basketball court, but he had a hard time getting the bigger college programs to notice him because he played for a small high school of around 150 students. Playing against some much bigger schools in Grand Rapids—and beating them—helped his cause, though. After leading his team to a 24–2 record and the state quarterfinals his senior year, Chris received a handful of scholarship offers, including one from Azusa Pacific University, a Christian college in Southern California.

Chris wanted to play close to home, so he accepted a full-ride offer from Central Michigan University in Mount Pleasant. A Division I school, CMU had a strong basketball program and was just seventy-five miles from his home. Over the next three years, his parents not only wouldn't miss a home game, they would also cheer him on at nearly all his road games.

Before leaving home to enroll at Central Michigan, however, Chris made a major decision that would change the arc of his life—he stopped taking his Adderall. It was his choice.

"In the summer of 2000, I was done taking my medicine," he said. "I didn't need my parents' permission because I was eighteen. When I told my parents what I wanted to do, they asked me to stay on my medicine. I explained I didn't want to do that. We got into a scuffle, but ultimately it was my choice."

After getting off the Adderall, Chris immediately began putting on some much-needed weight. During his freshman year in college, he quickly leaped to 214 pounds. His weight gain continued, and he steadily moved up to 225 pounds his sophomore year and tipped the scales at 237 pounds going into his junior year. By the time he started playing in the NBA, he was up to 255 pounds. No longer could heavier, more muscular centers push him around in the paint.

Chris' breakout season at Central Michigan came during

his junior year, when he doubled his point-per-game average to 22.4 and averaged 12 rebounds per game. During the 2002–03 season, he carried the Chippewas' hopes on his tall shoulders. An early season win at the University of Michigan raised eyebrows in the Great Lakes State. Chris scored 30 points and secured 21 rebounds in the victory at Ann Arbor.

Basketball was rocking again in Mount Pleasant. The student section in the east end zone—known as the Rose Rowdies because the Chippewas played in the Rose Arena—loved Chris, who led CMU to the NCAA Tournament for the first time since 1987.

Playing as an eleventh seed, Central Michigan stunned sixth-seeded Creighton in the first round of the West Regional played in Salt Lake City. The Chippewas had to hold off a furious second-half Creighton rally led by Kyle Korver, who scored 14 points in the second half to cut a 26-point lead to 2 late in the game.

Waiting in the second round was Duke University and Coach K—Mike Krzyzewski—whose Blue Devils were always one of the top teams in the country. Alas, Central Michigan was no match, losing 86–60. Chris played well, through, scoring 25 points and impressing Coach K.

"He can use both hands, and he can run the floor," Coach Krzyzewski said about Chris after the game. "If he gets fouled, he can hit free throws. He's going to be a pro; there's no doubt about it."

Since mobile, athletic 7-foot centers who can shoot don't come around too often, NBA scouts told Chris he should skip his senior season and turn pro because he was a certain first-round draft pick.

But was it the right time to leave Central Michigan to play in the NBA? His coach, Jay Smith, wanted Chris to come back for his senior year, but as Chris and his parents discussed their options, they felt the time was right to turn pro. "I have to do it now," Chris told his parents. "If Central Michigan doesn't do as well next year, the NBA will forget about me."

Chris decided to turn pro and was the sixth player taken in the 2003 NBA draft. The perennial doormat of the NBA—the Los Angeles Clippers—selected Chris, making him the highest draft pick of any athlete in any sport to come from Grand Rapids.

WESTWARD HO

And now Chris was in the NBA.

Playing at the next level presented its own challenges, not the least of which was leaving his home state and moving to Los Angeles. Chris made a good decision when he asked Ben Chamberlain, his older brother Michael's best friend at Tri-Unity, to be his personal assistant and keep his life in order. Ben was like a big brother to Chris.

Later in Chris' rookie season, Ben's younger brother Caleb, as well as Jeremy Scully, a friend of Michael's, also moved from Grand Rapids to LA to live with Chris and Ben. Jeremy, who had earned a degree at a culinary school, was put in charge of cooking for everyone at the home Chris purchased in Redondo Beach.

"They were all Christian guys who thought the same way I do," Chris said. "They were good people to surround myself with. They lived with me the whole time until I got married in 2010, but I had them around for two reasons: one was to make sure that I had people I knew and felt comfortable to hang out with. And two, I wanted them to be a barrier between me and anybody who wanted to befriend me to get to my money."

Before Ben was on board, Chris had been overly generous with his newfound riches. His first fifty thousand dollars was gone in a week and a half; he handed out hundred-dollar bills or wrote checks to friends and family members like he was passing out Monopoly money at a game table. After that, he voluntarily gave up his checkbook and restricted himself to a bank card that had a preset spending limit each day.

It helped that Chris had no desire to sample LA's night-life, and having a three-man posse to hang out with—and keep him accountable—helped him avoid temptations with the ladies.

"I liked my teammates, but I couldn't see myself doing some of the things they did," Chris said. "The hardest part about joining an NBA team was staying positive in my faith when people all around me were talking about stuff I didn't need to hear. Bad company robs good spirit, and I wanted to surround myself with good company."

Besides, with Jeremy's great food, tons of video games to play, and a pet Rottweiler at home, what more could four guys in their twenties living in LA's beach-centric west side want or need?

Chris and his buddies held Bible studies and went to church together. Ben sent two or three Bible verses a day to Chris' BlackBerry whenever he was on a road trip. Chris upped the ante by being vocal about his faith and telling reporters that he didn't consider himself a religious person but someone who wanted to be a good person who loved God.

Chris got a lot of media attention in Los Angeles when he won the Clippers' starting center position during his first training camp. He performed well his first few years in the NBA, although Clippers coach Mike Dunleavy wanted him to be more selfish with the ball. Chris would get the ball in the low post and have a close-in shot, but he'd pass off to a team-mate who would take a long-range jumper—and that player usually wasn't half the shooter Chris was.

Then Chris always seemed to be fighting ankle sprains and other nagging injuries—and a reputation that he wasn't all together during games. There were times when Coach Dunleavy would call time out and draw up a play for the next possession, and Chris would walk out of the huddle as the horn sounded. A second later, he'd turn around in a half panic and ask, "Coach, what play are we running again? I forgot already."

Not good, especially when you're down by one point with ten seconds left in the game.

The occasional bouts of forgetfulness led to whispers around the league that Chris was a flake—a space cadet on the court. His brain was still moving too fast, and he was missing stuff.

In 2007, after five up-and-down years in the league, Chris' uncle, Mike Palmitier, heard about a new company in Grand Rapids called Neurocore. Psychologists Dr. Tim Royer and his associate Dr. Brad Oostindie started Neurocore, which helped people find long-term, non-invasive, non-drug so-lutions to behavioral issues. Uncle Mike's teenage daughter

Torrie had used the program to improve her grades as well as her attitude around the home.

Chris was initially dubious when Uncle Mike told him about Neurocore, but he decided to check the company out. Neurocore technicians attached twenty-one electrodes to Chris' head so they could assess his brainwave activity. Using a system of neurofeedback, they were able to identify ways Chris could sharpen his focus, reduce stress, and make positive changes in the way his brain operates.

They also discovered that Chris *didn't* suffer from ADHD, despite what other doctors had told him and his parents.

"I was real skeptical about Neurocore," Chris said. "After being hooked up and having my brainwave activity assessed, they told me that I wasn't ADHD at all. What I had was high anxiety, and taking Ritalin made my high anxiety worse for all those years. That's why I always felt like I was crawling out of my skin and forgetting plays and coverages in my games."

In other words, Chris had been misdiagnosed since he was two-and-a-half years old! Dr. Royer at Neurocore suggested that Chris undergo Neurocore's Autonomic Nervous System Regulation (ANSR) program, which he did. The results were nothing short of amazing.

Since Chris completed the ANSR program, his game has really picked up. His best season was the 2009–10 season, when he averaged a career-high 18.5 points and 9.3 rebounds a game. A sprained ankle early in the 2010–11 season, however, limited him to 32 games, but he remained a huge advocate of Neurocore. "I've noticed a big difference in the way I play," he said. "I'm not so impulsive, and I can stay on task longer."

For the past few summers, Chris has traveled around the country giving talks before parents or doing teleconferences from Los Angeles and Grand Rapids on how Neurocore helped him understand what he was really up against and how Neurocore's technology showed him once and for all that he was *not* ADHD.

"When a kid is told he has ADHD, that usually comes after a doctor visit seven to ten minutes long," he said. "During that short amount of time, the doctor prescribes a strong medication that can change your life forever. This is why I'm out there talking to parents, saying, 'Don't be so quick to put your kids on medication. Maybe there is an alternative way to do it. Maybe your kid is not really ADHD.' "

How has that message been received?

"Sometimes it's good, and sometimes the parents are tired of battling their kid, so they say, 'Yeah, the doctor must be right.' But as I point out, doctors get paid money to put kids on medications. They get a bonus when they write scripts. So what I tell everybody is check out Neurocore first. What's it going to hurt?"

SPRECHEN SIE DEUTSCH?

Six months before the 2008 Olympics in Beijing, China, Chris Kaman and his buddy Dallas Mavericks star Dirk Nowitzki, talked about the upcoming Summer Games. Dirk, also a 7-footer, was born and raised in Würzburg, Germany, and was planning to play on Germany's Olympic basketball team. The pair discussed what kind of chance Germany had against a strong American team that was heavily favored to win the gold medal.

Chris, who was invited to try out for Team USA but wasn't selected, actually has some German blood running through his veins. He told Dirk that his great-grandparents immigrated to the United States from Germany just before the start of World War I.

As the two kept talking, they hatched a plan: based on his heritage, could Chris qualify for a German passport and play for Germany?

Chris was available.

"I was asked to be on the U.S. practice squad and scrimmage against the guys going to Beijing, but that wasn't the same as playing in the Olympics," Chris said. "The more I talked to Dirk about playing for Germany, the more I decided to just go for it. My dad's grandparents came over from Germany, and that was enough to get me a German passport."

The paperwork proved more daunting than expected. His application wasn't approved until June, just days before the qualifying games started.

He wasn't the only American-born NBA player on the German national team: Demond Greene, a 6-foot, 1-inch guard from Killeen, Texas, was also on the team. Demond qualified because he was the son of a U.S. serviceman who met his future wife, a German local, while stationed in Germany. Demond was the offspring of their union.

Chris knew what people were thinking when news got out that he would be playing for the Germans: *traitor*.

"I was an American, playing for Germany, so 'traitor' is the first thing that comes to your mind," Chris said. "I didn't care. I wanted to enjoy the entire Olympic experience, and I did. It was a once-in-a-lifetime thing, walking into the Bird's Nest for the opening ceremonies. Dirk held up the German flag, and I tried to take it all in. Walking around the track was unbelievable. I remember that it was so hot; it must have been

90 degrees and the humidity must have been 80 percent. All my clothes were drenched. When I walked by those 2,008 guys beating the drums, I wondered if this was really happening. It was just a cool opportunity, and I'm glad I got to play, even if it was for Germany."

If you're wondering how Chris—whose German vocabulary isn't much more than *ja* and *nein*—communicated with his teammates, he had no problems. All but two of the players spoke perfect English.

The German team won only one game out of five in Group B, defeating Angola. The United States defeated Spain in the gold medal game.

Will Chris play for Germany in the 2012 Olympics in London?

"If Dirk is ready to play, I'm ready to play," Chris said.

WEDDING BELLS

Chris met his future wife, Emilie, back at Central Michigan University, but they were not close in college and never dated.

One day in 2007, Chris was looking at his MySpace page—the social networking website in which he introduces himself by saying, "I love Jesus and basketball"—and noticed that Emilie had posted a hello.

Chris responded with his own message: "Hey, what's going on? What have you been up to?"

He learned that Emilie was in Phoenix, and they kept messaging back and forth. One time, when Emilie was in LA, they had lunch together, and things progressed from there.

Did any of Chris' teammates find out he was seeing Emilie?

"I kind of kept it on the down low because I wasn't sure if it was going to work out or not. I had been real skeptical of girls in the past—skeptical that nothing ever worked out before. A lot of girls you don't know about because you don't know them," he said, sounding like he was doing his best imitation of Yogi Berra. "But if you know someone from before, you feel more comfortable with her."

He even kept their budding love story secret from his family for a while.

Chris and Emilie dated for three years before Chris asked her to marry him in 2010. They had a wonderful wedding in Kauai in June, where they also honeymooned.

But what happened to his posse after Chris and Emilie returned from their Hawaii honeymoon? After all, two's a couple and three (or more) are a crowd.

"Ben and Caleb Chamberlain moved back to Michigan, and Jeremy Scully is now my personal assistant/chef/business manager. He's renting an apartment near our home in Manhattan Beach. Now we have this huge house just for Emilie and me, and that feels kind of weird," Chris said.

"Maybe we'll fill up the house with kids someday."

HE'S A WILD AND CRAZY GUY

Chris Kaman has always marched to the beat of a different drummer. When he turned pro and signed a multi-million-dollar deal, he treated himself to a car—a '72 Chevelle. He drove that heap for many years before buying a used Mercedes that allows him to stretch his feet.

Chris, who hunted a lot growing up in Michigan, is also an avid collector of guns and knives. One summer a few years ago, back home in Michigan, he purchased a junkyard '88 Ford Taurus for fifty dollars and had it hauled to his parents' property. (One of the first things Chris did after signing with the Clippers was build his parents a new home on twenty-four acres outside Grand Rapids.)

Then he and his buddies spent a summer afternoon firing .50-caliber shells from a semi-automatic Barrett rifle. Each round was bigger than a giant-sized Tootsie Roll and cost five dollars. "We shot five clips that day—fifty shots."

Just type in "Chris Kaman and guns" into a YouTube search, and you can watch Chris and buddies take out the defenseless Taurus.

5

JEREMY LIN:
A STORY HOLLYWOOD WOULD
HAVE TROUBLE BELIEVING

Here's an e-mail I'd love to write someday:

> **To:** bigshotproducer@hollywoodstudio.com
> **From:** mike@mikeyorkey.com
> **Subject:** Jeremy Lin pitch
> Hollywood has a long tradition of producing "feel good" sports movies about athletes who overcome rejection, author the unexpected come-from-behind victory, or triumph by making the team, winning the champion-ship, or going the distance against all odds. I'm thinking of films like *Rudy*, *Invincible*, *The Blind Side*, and *Rocky I*, *II*, *III*, *IV*, and *V*. Sure, they're formulaic, but conquering hardship,

adversity, and life's bad breaks is the key plot point for any of these movies.

I have an underdog story that would be a surefire winner at the box office, and it's rather unbelievable, even by Hollywood standards. Better yet, the story of Jeremy Lin—arguably the first Asian-American to play in the NBA— is 100 percent true.

Can we do lunch next week?

I'm not sure what kind of response I'd get to my Jeremy Lin "elevator pitch," but I'm confident that if I sat across the table from a Hollywood mover-and-shaker, I could walk away with a green light for the Jeremy Lin project. The improbable story of how a Taiwanese immigrant's son overcame preconceived ideas about who can and can't play basketball at the highest level has the necessary elements to emotionally move audiences.

There are plenty of entry points for a film about Jeremy Lin, but a good place to start would be by painting a picture of China in the late 1940s, when civil war ripped apart the world's most populous country. Chinese Nationalist forces led by General Chiang Kai-shek fought the People's Liberation Army—led by Chinese Communist Party leader Mao Zedong—for control of China, which, at that time, was a feudal society where a small elite class lived well and hundreds of millions barely survived. In 1949, after three years of bloody conflict, the Communist forces won, and Chiang Kai-shek and approximately two million Nationalist Chinese fled for their lives to the island of Taiwan off the coast of mainland China.

Among those refugees were Jeremy's grandparents on his mother's side. Shirley Lin ("Shirley" is actually an anglicized version of her Chinese first name) was born to a mother who was one of Taiwan's first prominent female physicians. One time during the 1970s, a contingent of American doctors visited Taiwan to study the advances Taiwanese physicians were making in health care. As Shirley's mother made contacts with those in the American medical community, the seed was planted to immigrate to the United States, where the family could pursue a better life. In 1978, just after Shirley graduated from high school in Taiwan, she and the family moved to the United States.

Shirley worked hard learning English and later enrolled at Old Dominion University, a college in Norfolk, Virginia. Her major was computer science, a discipline with a bright future. Many felt the computer revolution would explode in the 1980s. A newfangled invention called the PC, or personal computer, was starting to find its way into American homes.

There weren't too many Asians (or second-generation Asian-Americans, for that matter) at Old Dominion, and those who spoke Mandarin could be counted on two hands. The dozen or so Chinese-speaking students formed a small Asian support group for fun and fellowship, and one of those who joined was a graduate student from Taiwan—a handsome young man named Gie-Ming Lin, who'd come to the United States to work on his doctorate in computer engineering. His ancestors had lived in Taiwan since the nineteenth century, long before Communist oppression began on the mainland in the late 1940s and early 1950s.

Sharing the same cultural background and a common

language brought Gie-Ming and Shirley together, and they
began dating. It wasn't long before their love blossomed.
When Gie-Ming told her that his plan was to finish his doctorate at Purdue University in West Lafayette, Indiana, they
decided to move together to Purdue, where Shirley would
continue her undergraduate classes in computer science
while Gie-Ming worked on his PhD.

Don't get the idea that these two foreign-born students
had plenty of time to linger over coffees at the student union,
attend a concert at the Elliott Hall of Music, or go sledding
down Slayter Hill after the first snowfall of winter. Gie-Ming
and Shirley's parents didn't have the financial resources to
contribute to their education, so they both had to work to
pay their own tuition and living expenses. Shirley took shifts
waitressing and bartending, while Gie-Ming moonlighted in
his chosen field of computer engineering.

While at Purdue, Shirley was introduced to a Christian
fellowship group, and she heard the Gospel presented for the
first time. Curious about who Jesus was, she began explor-
ing and learning about the Lord of the universe and how He
came to this earth to die for her sins. She fell in love with
Christ and got saved. When she told Gie-Ming what she had
done, he investigated the Gospel and became a Christian as
well. They soon plugged into a Chinese-speaking church and
began their walk with Christ.

Gie-Ming and Shirley married while they were still in
school. They liked living in the United States and became two of
the many millions of immigrants chasing the American dream.

They certainly weren't afraid to work hard—or live fru-
gally. Early on, Gie-Ming and Shirley would go fishing on

the weekend at a nearby reservoir. Behind the dam was a lake teeming with bluegill, shad, crappie, and huge bass. Gie-Ming, who loved fishing and was quite good at it, would catch his limit and then bring home his haul in a galvanized bucket. They ate some of the fish that night and tossed the rest into the freezer.

And that's how the young couple would feed themselves all week long—from the fish Gie-Ming caught on weekends.

One evening, Gie-Ming flipped on the television to relax, and he came across a basketball game. The Lakers were playing the Celtics during one of their great 1980s NBA Finals playoff series, and the sight of Bird and Magic doing wondrous things on the Boston Garden parquet floor mesmerized Gie-Ming. He was smitten by the athleticism of these larger-than-life figures who made the basketball court look small. Gie-Ming started watching NBA basketball every chance he had, but that wasn't often since his studies and part-time work took up much of his free time.

Wait! Wasn't there a new technology arriving in people's homes back then? Yes, it was called the VHS recorder, and this then-state-of-the-art electromechanical device could record television broadcasts on cassettes that contained magnetic tape. Suddenly, the images and sound of TV shows and sporting events could be played back at a more convenient time—or replayed over and over for the viewer's enjoyment. The advent of the VHS tape in the 1980s revolutionized the way Gie-Ming—and millions of Americans—watched TV.

Gie-Ming started taping NBA games, and he loved watching Kareem's sky hook, Dr. J's gravity-defying dunks, and Magic leading the fast break and handling the ball like it was on the end of a string. It wasn't long before Gie-Ming was a certifiable basketball junkie. He studied those tapes with the same fervor as when he studied for his PhD. He couldn't tell friends *why* he loved basketball, but he just did.

Gie-Ming also started playing a bit of basketball himself. He taught himself how to dribble and how to shoot by practicing jump shot after jump shot at a nearby playground. He was too shy to join a basketball league, but he could be coaxed into playing the occasional pickup game. He loved breaking a sweat on the basketball court, and playing the game became his favorite form of exercise.

When Gie-Ming and Shirley completed their schooling at Purdue, they moved to Los Angeles, where Gie-Ming worked for a company that designed microchips. Shirley jumped on the mommy track and gave birth to their first child, a son they named Joshua. Two years later, on August 23, 1988, ten years to the day after Kobe Bryant entered the world in Philadelphia, Jeremy Shu-How Lin was born.

WHAT'S WITH THE *J*'S AND *K*'S?

Jeremy Lin and Kyle Korver share more than their basketball prowess in common. They were both born in the 1980s in Los Angeles into all-sons families. Whereas Kyle is the oldest of four boys whose names all started with the letter *K*—Kyle, Klayton, Kaleb, and Kirk—Jeremy comes from a family where Mom and Dad gave their three sons names starting with the letter *J*: Joshua, Jeremy, and Joseph.

A job offer moved the family to Florida for two years, but then Silicon Valley lured Gie-Ming and Shirley to Northern

California in the early 1990s. Gie-Ming's expertise became computer chip design, while Shirley—who had given birth to her third son, Joseph—returned to work in her specialty, quality control, which meant making sure new computer programs were bug-free when they were released.

Silicon Valley, in the southern part of the San Francisco Bay Area, was home to many of the world's largest technology corporations. No, the Lins didn't work for Apple or Google, which was still the brainchild of a pair of Stanford computer science grad students named Larry Page and Sergey Brin, but the Lins had good jobs at high-tech firms. They arrived at Silicon Valley at a fortuitous time and paddled into a cresting wave of technology-driven products that would soon change the way we live, interact, and process information.

The Lins settled in Palo Alto, a community of sixty thousand residents that bordered Stanford University. Gie-Ming, who wanted to introduce his favorite game—basketball—to his boys, signed up for a family membership at the local YMCA. (You can be sure that James Naismith would have been very pleased.) When firstborn Joshua was five years old, Gie-Ming introduced him to the fundamentals of basketball by using the passing, dribbling, and shooting drills he'd studied on his VHS tapes. Jeremy received the same instruction when he started kindergarten, and so would Joseph when he reached that age.

When Jeremy entered first grade, his parents signed him up for a youth basketball league. But at that young age, Jeremy wasn't very interested in the action around him. He was like those kids in T-ball who lay down on the outfield grass and watch the clouds pass by instead of what the next batter is going to do. Most of the time, Jeremy stood at half-court and sucked his thumb while the ball went up and down the floor. Since he couldn't be bothered to try harder, his mom stopped coming to his games.

As Jeremy grew and matured, he eventually became more interested in basketball, especially after he grew big enough to launch an effective shot toward the rim and watch it swish through the net. As shot after shot poured through the hoop, he was hooked. He asked his mother if she would come back and watch him play, but she wanted to know if he was actually going to try before she committed to returning to his games.

"You watch," he promised. "I'm going to play, and I'm going to score."

He scored all right. Sometimes Jeremy scored the maximum amount of points one player was allowed to under biddy basketball rules.

For the rest of Jeremy's elementary school years, his parents regularly took him and his brothers to the gym to practice or play in pickup games. They also enrolled him in youth soccer, but basketball was the game he wanted to play.

As the demands of schoolwork grew, Jeremy and his brothers would do their homework after school, wait for their father to come home for dinner, and then everyone would head over to the Y at eight o'clock for ninety minutes of shooting and pickup games. Gie-Ming continued to stress the fundamentals because he wanted the game's basic moves to become second nature to Jeremy.

As Jeremy improved, he couldn't get enough hoops action. On many nights, he and his family practiced and played right up until the time they closed the doors at the Palo Alto Family YMCA at 9:45 p.m.

CHURCH AND BASKETBALL

While basketball turned out to be a fun family sport for the Lins, they weren't going to sacrifice academics or church on the altar of basketball. Academics were important to Gie-Ming and Shirley because they had seen firsthand how education could give them a better life. Church was even more important because they knew what a relationship with Christ meant to them and to the spiritual well-being of their sons.

Wherever they lived, the Lins gravitated toward a Chinese Christian church. When they moved to Palo Alto, they found a church they immediately liked: the Chinese Church in Christ in nearby Mountain View. This place of worship was really two churches in one. There were two services every Sunday at 11:00 a.m.—one in Mandarin and the other in English—in separate fellowship halls. Usually two hundred or so attended the Mandarin-speaking service, while around a hundred attended the worship service presented in English.

The strong demand for a church service in Mandarin was reflective of the demographics of the San Francisco Bay Area, home to the nation's highest concentration of Asian-Americans. At one time, the U.S. Census revealed that 27 percent of the people living in Pala Alto were Asian-Americans—racially identifying themselves as Chinese-American, Filipino-American, Korean-American, Japanese-American, or Vietnamese-American. There was a large Taiwanese-American community in nearby Cupertino (24 percent of the population), while other bedroom communities like Millbrae, Foster City, Piedmont, and Albany had Asian populations of 10 percent or greater.

Stephen Chen, pastor of the Chinese Church of Christ,

remembers the first time he met Jeremy ten years ago, when Chen was the youth counselor. "Jeremy was around thirteen when I first ran into him," he said. "We were having a church cleaning day, and he was running around with his friends and being rambunctious. I remember scolding him, saying, 'Hey, we're trying to clean things up, and you're making things more messy.'"

Feeling chastised, Jeremy went home and told his parents he didn't want to go to that church anymore because the youth guy had been so mean to him. His parents didn't take his side, however, and the incident soon blew over.

Stephen Chen, looking for things to do with the youth in the church, discovered that Jeremy and his older brother Josh were avid basketball players. Josh was starting to play high school basketball, and Jeremy was living and breathing the game in middle school.

"I hadn't played a lick of basketball before that time," Stephen said. "But I wanted to connect with the Lin brothers, so I asked them if we could do a little exchange: I would teach them about the Bible and they would teach me how to play basketball."

Josh and Jeremy readily accepted. After youth group was over, they'd go to a nearby basketball court, where the Lin brothers taught Stephen how to do a lay-up, properly shoot the ball, and box out on rebounds. Then they would get the youth group together, choose up sides, and play basketball games.

"Jeremy would pass me the ball, even when the game was on the line," Stephen said. "He wasn't afraid that I'd lose the game for him. If we did lose, his older brother would get upset, but Jeremy would even console his brother. Even at that young age, Jeremy was hospitable, eager to get along with different types of people. He was also a natural leader, and kids listened to him."

Before entering high school, Jeremy wanted to get baptized as a public statement that he believed in Jesus Christ as his Lord and Savior. Stephen was pleased to hear of that desire. The Chinese Church of Christ had a baptismal inside the church sanctuary, and Jeremy was dunked during a Sunday morning service. Not long after that, Stephen asked him if he'd become part the youth ministry's leadership team.

Jeremy was willing. The church had been renting out a local high school gym on Sunday evenings so the kids in the youth group could play basketball and invite their friends to join them. "Jeremy would always be the one who would ask other kids to come out and play basketball with us," Stephen said. "And they would come. Jeremy wanted everyone to feel at home. That was just another way how he extended kindness to others."

The gym had two full courts across the main court. Many dads saw how much fun their kids were having, so they would play, too—fathers on one court and their sons on the other. Moms would visit with each other during the games of roundball.

All this basketball playing—after school, on weekends, and on Sunday nights—helped Jeremy to become quite a player, even though he was a shrimp on the court. As he entered his freshman year of high school, Jeremy topped out at 5 feet, 3 inches tall and weighed 125 pounds. Jeremy had set his sights on playing high school basketball, but he knew that if he didn't grow a lot in the next couple of years, he wasn't going to get a chance to play, no matter how talented he was.

One day, Jeremy told Stephen, "I want to be at least six feet tall."

Stephen looked at Jeremy. He knew that Asians were stereotyped as a short people, and there was some truth to that. The average male height in the United States is 5 feet, 10 inches, while in China, the average male height is 5 feet, 7 inches. Unfortunately for Jeremy, his parents weren't tall either. Both stood 5 feet, 6 inches, so he didn't have a great gene pool working for him. (The 7-foot, 6-inch Yao Ming of China did—see the sidebar.)

"So how are you going to become six feet tall?" Stephen asked.

"I'm going to drink milk every day," young Jeremy replied.

For the next few years, Shirley was constantly running to the local supermarket to buy milk by the gallon. He drank the dairy product like it was . . . water. Jeremy had a glass of milk with his breakfast cereal, drank milk at lunch, and always had a couple more glasses of milk with dinner.

"I drank so much milk because I was obsessed with my height," Jeremy said. "I'd wake up in the morning and measure myself every day because I heard that you're always taller in the morning, at least when you're growing. I wanted to see if I had grown overnight."

Jeremy's great wish was to be taller than his older brother, Josh, who was in the midst of a growth spurt that would take him to 5 feet, 10 inches during high school. Desperate to will his body to grow taller, Jeremy even climbed on monkey bars at school and let himself hang upside down, thinking that would expand his spinal column and make him taller.

Kyle Korver, one of the best spot-up shooters in the game, fires over the Indiana Pacers' Brandon Rush during a playoff game. The Chicago Bulls advanced to the 2010–11 NBA Finals against the Miami Heat but lost in five games.

Not too many NBA centers can get a hand on the ball when 7-foot, 6-inch Yao Ming goes to the hoop, but Los Angeles Clipper Chris Kaman—giving up six inches as a seven-footer—timed this blocked shot perfectly.

Ric Francis, Associated Press

Anthony Parker defends former teammate LeBron James in a game played during the 2010–11 season in Miami. Parker played five years in Israel for Maccabi Tel Aviv before returning to the NBA in 2009.

Keith Srakocic, Associated Press

Luke Ridnour whips a no-look pass in a game against the Utah Jazz during a game from the 2010–11 season. Growing up in the small town of Blaine, Washington, Ridnour idolized Pistol Pete Maravich and his amazing passing and dribbling skills.

Jeremy Lin glides past several Utah Jazz defenders during his rookie season in 2010–11. Lin is arguably the first Asian-American to play in the NBA.

Steve C. Wilson, Associated Press

Stephen Curry protects the ball against New Orleans. Former coaches and mentors of Curry say that he displays Christ-honoring character and "humble superstar spirit" when he plays.

Patrick Semansky, Associated Press

Nenê—that's his full name—drives to the basket. The Brazilian power forward/center, who is a massive presence on the court for the Denver Nuggets, has his eye on church ministry back in his home country when his NBA career is over.

Barry Gutierrez, Associated Press

Reggie Williams slashes to the hoop as well as anyone and can "quietly" score 20 points on any evening. The former NCAA scoring leader for two seasons plays alongside Jeremy Lin for the Golden State Warriors.

Jim Urquhart, Associated Press

Nick Collison of the Oklahoma City Thunder is one of those lunch-pail players who'll take the charge or stand his ground in the paint. Here he rejects a shot by the Dallas Mavericks' Jason Terry during a 2010–11 playoff game.

Tony Gay, Associated Press

Kevin Durant is one of the NBA's rising stars with a game that's a mixture of grace, class, and force. Already a two-time scoring leader, some say this face of the Oklahoma City Thunder franchise could become the greatest scorer in NBA history.

Alonzo Adams, Associated Press

Greivis Vasquez, who hails from Venezuela, flips a shot past a defender on this drive to the basket. Vasquez has taken to Twitter and tweets about going to church and his love for Christ.

Mark J. Terrill, Associated Press

Jeremy understood that he couldn't "force" his body to grow, but he also believed that to be competitive in the game of basketball, he had to grow to at least six feet tall.

YAO MING: BRED FOR GREATNESS

When American basketball fans think of Asians playing the game, their first thought goes to Yao Ming, the 7-foot, 6-inch center for the Houston Rockets. Yao isn't the tallest player ever to play in the NBA—7-foot, 7-inch Manute Bol and Gheorghe Muresan share that distinction—but he's almost half a foot taller than Pau Gasol, Dirk Nowitzki, and Shaquille O'Neal—and Kareem Abdul-Jabbar and Wilt Chamberlain, for that matter. Although Yao's missed the last two seasons with nagging foot and ankle problems, he's still the face of basketball in Asia.

There are strong indications that Chinese athletic officials strongly "encouraged" the marriage of two of their basketball stars—a 6-foot, 9-inch man, Yao Zhiyuan, and a 6-foot, 3-inch woman, Fang Fengdi—with the hopes that they would successfully produce a basketball center like the world had never seen. Not much was left to chance in the Chinese communist sports system, where doctors traveled around the country measuring youngsters' bones and torsos to identify future athletes. Weight lifters must be squat with strong midsections, divers need tiny hips to minimize splash, and basketball players must be *really* tall.

Fang Fengdi, the captain of China's women's basketball team who had been a feared member of the Red Guard during the murderous Cultural Revolution, readily agreed to the grand experiment proposed by Chinese sports officials. The pairing of giants produced only one child, however, and one can surmise Mama Fang had second thoughts about going through childbirth a second time after the excruciatingly difficult delivery of an eleven-pound boy who was nearly double the size of the average Chinese newborn.

As far as the Chinese basketball federation was concerned, Yao Ming's birth was just the beginning. They saw to it that Yao was given growth supplements to make him even taller, and when he was eight years old, they put him into a sports school, where he would practice five afternoons a week and on Saturdays. Yao hated being forced to play basketball, but he resigned himself to practice out of respect for his parents.

Although he loathed the game for a long time and wasn't a very good player until his late teens, Yao Ming—like a giraffe finding its legs—eventually discovered his game. Now, at the age of thirty-one, Yao has decided that his brittle body will not allow him to make a comeback. He retired prior to the start of the 2011–12 season, which means we won't get to see him play against Jeremy Lin and the Golden State Warriors.

Can you imagine the exorbitant scalper's prices to see that game in the Bay Area?

MIRACLE-GRO

Jeremy enrolled at Palo Alto High School, where he made a big impression on his freshman basketball coach—even though he was one of the smallest players on the team. Years of playing in youth basketball leagues at the Y had honed his skills. His freshman coach stood up at the team's end-of-the-season banquet and declared, "Jeremy has a better skill set than anyone I've seen at his age."

And then something miraculous happened.

Jeremy grew.

And grew.

And grew.

By Jeremy's junior year, he had sprouted *nine inches* to

reach the magic number—six feet of height. But he wasn't done. Jeremy would go on to add two more inches by his senior year and another inch or inch and a half in college to reach his present height, which is a tad over 6 feet, 3 inches. He also added bulk: his body filled out to a solid 200 pounds.

Not only did Jeremy grow like a beanstalk during his freshman and sophomore years, but he also showed Palo Alto High opponents that he could run the offense, shoot lights-out, and make the player he was guarding work extra hard. His position was point guard, which is perhaps the most specialized role in basketball. The point guard is expected to lead the team's half-court offense, run the fast break, make the right pass at the right time, work the pick-and-roll, and penetrate the defense, which creates open teammates when he gets double-teamed.

When Jeremy dribbled the ball into the front court, he played like a quarterback who approached the line of scrim-mage and scanned the defense to determine its vulnerabili-ties as well as its capabilities. Jeremy's mind quickly deter-mined how an opponent's defense was set up and where the weak spots were. His quickness and mobility were assets.

During his sophomore season, Jeremy was not only good enough to win the point guard starting role, but his fantas-tic play also earned him the first of three first-team All-Santa Clara Valley Athletic League awards. During his junior season, he was the driving force behind Palo Alto High, helping the team set a school record for victories by posting a 32–2 record.

It was during Jeremy's senior year that he was the mo-tor that propelled his team to the Division II California state championship. Going into the championship game, Palo

Alto was a huge underdog against perennial powerhouse Mater Dei, a Catholic high school from Santa Ana in Southern California. No team had won more state basketball titles than Mater Dei, and the Monarchs, who had a 32–2 record, came into the game ranked among the nation's top teams.

Talk about a David-versus-Goliath matchup. Mater Dei was loaded with Division I recruits and had eight players 6 feet, 7 inches or taller, while Palo Alto had no one over 6 feet, 6 inches. Playing at Arco Arena, home of the Sacramento Kings, Jeremy was all over the court and personally engineered the plucky and undersized Palo Alto team to a two-point lead with two minutes to play. Could the Vikings hang on?

Jeremy brought the offense up the floor, trying to eat up as much clock as possible. Suddenly, there were just seconds left on the 35-second shot clock. Jeremy was above the top of the key when he launched a rainbow toward the rim to beat the shot clock buzzer. The ball banked in, giving Palo Alto a five-point lead.

Mater Dei wasn't finished yet, and neither was Jeremy. The Monarchs cut the lead to 2 points with 30 seconds to go, and then Jeremy dribbled the ball into the front court. Mater Dei didn't want to foul him because the Monarchs knew he was an excellent free throw shooter, so they waited for him to dish off to a teammate. Jeremy, however, sensed an opening and drove to the basket in a flash, taking on Mater Dei's star player, 6-foot, 8-inch Taylor King, in the paint. Jeremy went up and over King for a lay-up that gave him a total of 17 points in the game and iced the state championship in the 51–47 win.

You'd think that with all the college scouts in the stands for a state championship game, Jeremy would have to go into the Federal Witness Protection Program just to get a moment's respite. But the recruiting interest had been underwhelming all season long and stayed that way after the win over Mater Dei. It wasn't like Jeremy played for a tumbleweed-strewn high school in the middle of the Nevada desert. He was part of a respected program at Palo Alto High, and his coach, Peter Diepenbrock, was well-known to college coaches.

And Jeremy was highly regarded in Northern California high school basketball circles. He was named first-team All-State and Northern California's Division II Scholar Athlete of the Year. The *San Francisco Chronicle* newspaper named him Boys Player of the Year, as did the *San Jose Mercury News* and *Palo Alto Daily News*.

Despite all the great ink and the bushel basket of post-season awards, despite sending out a DVD of highlights a friend at church had prepared, and despite Coach Diepenbrock's lobbying efforts with college coaches, Jeremy did not receive *any* scholarship offers to play at a Division I school. That MIA list included Stanford University, which was located literally across the street from Palo Alto High. (A wide boulevard named El Camino Real separates the two schools.)

You'd think Stanford would have given Jeremy a good look. After all, Jeremy had checked off a lot of boxes for the Cardinal:

- great high school basketball résumé
- local product
- strong academic record
- Asian-American

Regarding the last bullet point, almost 20 percent of the undergrad Stanford student body was Asian-American, and, as you read earlier, the school was located in a part of the country with a strong Asian population. But the Stanford basketball program took a pass. Some Stanford boosters interceded for Jeremy, telling the coaches that they had to give this Lin kid a look. But the best response the family received was that Jeremy could always try to make the team as a walk-on.

The Lins' eyes turned across the bay toward Berkeley, but the University of California coaching staff said the same thing: *You can try to walk on, but no guarantees.* During one recruiting visit, a Cal coach called Jeremy "Ron."

The disrespect continued at Jeremy's dream school— UCLA, where Josh was enrolled. Jeremy would have loved to have played for the storied Bruin program, and he was the kind of upstanding young man legendary Bruin coach John Wooden would have recruited back in the 1960s and 1970s. But the message from UCLA coaches was the same: *You'll have to make the team as a walk-on.*

Jeremy knew that few walk-ons—non-scholarship players invited to try out for the team—ever stick on the Division I basketball roster. He would never say it himself, but some basketball observers thought the fact that Jeremy *was* Asian-American cost him a Division I scholarship. Recruiters couldn't look past his ethnicity, couldn't imagine an Asian-looking kid having the game to compete against the very best players in the country. For whatever reason, they couldn't picture him playing basketball at the Pac-10 level.

Jeremy had run into a "system" that blocked his path like two Shaqs in the paint. College coaches, who are the decision makers, look for something quantifiable in a high school player—like how tall he is or how high he can jump or how many points per game he scores. Jeremy's greatest strengths didn't show up in a box score. His game was running the show, leading the offense, and setting up teammates. He had an incredible feel for the game, a Magic-like peripheral vision, and a take-charge attitude that coaches love to see in their point guards.

"He knew exactly what needed to be done at every point in the basketball game," said Coach Diepenbrock. "He was able to exert his will on basketball games in ways you would not expect. It was just hard to quantify his fearlessness."

The problem likely stemmed from the fact that major college coaches had never recruited a standout Asian player before, so they didn't know what to do with Jeremy. Asian-American gym rats like him were a novelty in college basketball; only one out of every two hundred Division I basketball players came from Asian-American households. In many coaches' minds, college basketball stars had a different skin complexion or looked different than Jeremy.

The family had some options, however, thanks to Gie-Ming's and Shirley's insistence that their sons study and perform just as well in the classroom as they did on the basketball court. Jeremy carried a 4.2 grade point average (in the grade-point system, an A is worth 4 points, but AP or Advanced Placement classes were weighted heavier because of their difficulty) at Palo Alto High, where he had scored a perfect 800 on his SAT II Math 2C during his *freshman* year. He was editor of the school newspaper and would earn Palo Alto High's President's Award upon graduation. Jeremy's parents felt that if

Pac-10 and other Division I teams didn't want their son, then maybe he could play for a top-ranked academic college—like Harvard.

The Lins looked east—toward the eight Ivy League schools, which are the most selective (and therefore elite) universities in the country. Harvard and Brown each stepped up; both coaches said they'd guarantee him a roster spot. Each made the case that they *really* wanted him to play for their basketball programs.

In the Lin family, there was no discussion. If Harvard— the assumed No. 1 school in the country in nearly everyone's eyes—wanted him, then he was going to play basketball for Harvard, even if that meant his parents would pay for his schooling out of their own pockets. That was because Harvard, like Yale, Princeton, Columbia, and the rest of the Ivy League schools, didn't offer athletic scholarships.

This was no small consideration. In round numbers, a year of undergraduate studies at Harvard costs fifty thousand dollars, which covers tuition, room and board, books, fees, and the like. The Lins were already shelling out for Josh's education at UCLA.

"The tuition is nuts," Jeremy said. "My parents did everything they could to get me through school. I received some financial aid from Harvard and took some loans out."

It turned out to be a great investment.

BY THE NUMBERS

18: The number of Asian-American men's players in Division I college basketball (0.4 percent). This was according to the 2009 NCAA Race and Ethnicity Report, which was released when Jeremy Lin was playing basketball at Harvard.

23: The number of students at Harvard with the last name of Lin while Jeremy was playing.

DEALING WITH THE YAHOOS

Harvard basketball dates back to 1900, when John Kirkland Clark, a Harvard Law School student, introduced the game to the school. Basketball at Harvard, and at other colleges around the country, changed during the next century, and one telling example is the student section. You don't have to be studying to become a rocket scientist to know that college basketball crowds can be brutal.

When the student section is not rhythmically chanting "bull@#$%, bull@#$%" after a call they don't like, they're dressing up in ways that mock the other team—such as wearing the clothes of Mormon missionaries (white short-sleeved shirts, black pants, thin black ties, and black bike helmets) whenever Brigham Young University plays on the road.

San Diego State fans gave Brigham Young's sharpshooting guard, Jimmer Fredette, the full treatment during his senior year. One fan held up a sign that asked, "Which wife gave you mono?" in reference to Fredette's bout with mononucleosis earlier in his senior season. But that was tame compared to the mean-spirited "You're still Mormon!" chants from the student section.

So it should come as no surprise that the sight of a prominent, all-over-the-floor Asian-American basketball player personally *beating* their team would prompt a few immature—and likely drunk—members of student sections to taunt Jeremy during his four-year playing career at Harvard.

Some yelled really stupid (and racist) stuff, like "Hey, sweet and sour pork" or "wonton soup" from the stands. "Go back to China" and "The orchestra is on the other side of campus" were some of the other dim-witted taunts. One time at Georgetown, Jeremy heard terribly unkind remarks aimed in his direction, including the racial slurs "chink" and "slant eyes."

Jeremy just showed God's grace and gave his tormenters the other cheek. But he also played harder. Granted, the taunts bothered him at first, but he decided to let his game speak for itself. In the process, he helped make Harvard relevant again in college basketball.

Even Harvard's erudite professors would have a hard time coming up with superlatives to describe what Jeremy Lin meant to Harvard basketball. He certainly helped revive the program by providing outstanding floor leadership. He scored, he rebounded, and he dished. During his junior and senior years, he was the only NCAA Division I men's basketball player who ranked in the top 10 in his conference for scoring, rebounding, assists, steals, blocked shots, field goal percentage, free throw percentage, and three-point shooting percentage.

Was there anything missing? Well, he was co-leader of a campus Bible study group, so maybe there was a "souls saved" category that didn't get counted.

Jeremy Lin was a hit at Harvard, pure and simple. Some Harvard fans wore crimson red T-shirts with the words "Welcome to the Jeremy Lin Show" silk-screened across their backs. He achieved such notoriety that Santa Clara University, which is located fifteen miles from Palo Alto, invited the Harvard team to the West Coast for a "homecoming" game during Jeremy's senior year and sold out its 4,700-seat arena.

The East Coast media heard of the Jeremy Lin Show and sent reporters from New York and Boston to write about him. Some of the more memorable quotes:

- "Jeremy Lin is probably one of the best players in the country you don't know about" (ESPN's Rece Davis).

- "He is a joy to watch. He's smooth, smart, unselfish, and sees the floor like no one else on it sees" (*Boston Herald* columnist Len Megliola).

- "Keep an eye on Harvard's Jeremy Lin. The fact that he's an Asian-American guard playing at Harvard has probably kept him off the NBA radar too long. But as scouts are hunting everywhere for point guards, more and more are coming back and acknowledging that Lin is a legit prospect" (ESPN NBA draft analyst Chad Ford).

Jeremy's stock rose during his senior year when Harvard played then No. 12–ranked University of Connecticut, a traditional college basketball powerhouse, on the road. He dissected and bisected UConn for 30 points and nine rebounds and threw a scare into one of the top teams in the country. Harvard lost 79–73.

When Jeremy's playing career at Harvard was over, he had high hopes that an NBA team would draft him and give him a clean shot at making the roster. But then . . . God had another plan because the way Jeremy made it to the NBA only could have happened in God's economy. In other words, it was a miracle.

Let's review what happened.

After pre-draft workouts with eight teams, including his hometown Golden State Warriors, Jeremy was passed over through two rounds and sixty players chosen in the 2010 NBA draft. Playing at an Ivy League school probably had a lot to do with that—the last Harvard player to wear an NBA jersey was Ed Smith, who played all of eleven games in his one-season career back in 1953–54. The conventional wisdom among pro scouts was that Harvard players never pan out in the NBA.

After the draft, Dallas general manager Donnie Nelson invited Jeremy to play on the Mavericks' Summer League team. NBA Summer League games are played at frenetic pace, and they can be a bit sloppy, but for rookies or other non-roster players like Jeremy, summer league provides a fleeting chance—perhaps a *last* chance—to pit their skills against NBA-level players and make an impression. The eight-day summer league season was held in Las Vegas in July 2010.

Jeremy wasn't a starter for the Maverick Summer League team, not by a long shot. He sat behind an electrifying point guard named Rodrigue Beaubois, whom Dallas coaches were appraising for a roster spot. In the first four summer league games, Jeremy was a spot substitute who averaged just seventeen minutes and 8 points a game.

And then something happened that changed the arc of Jeremy's basketball life. Look for the hand of God through this series of events:

1. Jeremy's team was playing the Washington Wizards Summer League team, which featured John Wall, the No. 1 overall draft pick in the 2010 NBA

draft. Wall would be named the summer league MVP that season.

2. This was the last contest of the five-game summer league season. A large number of scouts and NBA team officials were on hand.

3. Rodrigue Beaubois had twisted an ankle and had a poor outing in the first half. Jeremy took his place.

4. By all accounts, Jeremy outplayed, outhustled, outdrove, and outshined John Wall in the second half while leading his team to a big comeback— drawing oohs and ahs from the crowd with several fearless drives to the rim.

Here's a thumbnail description of how Jeremy played: during the fourth quarter, Jeremy's tenacious defense on Wall forced a jump ball. He then came out of nowhere to make a sensational steal, then tore a rebound out of the hands of a 7-foot center. For the game, he hit six-of-twelve shots, including his only three-point try of the night.

Here's the clincher: after that single half of brilliant play, several NBA teams looked at Jeremy in a new light. The Mavericks, the Los Angeles Lakers, and the Golden State Warriors all saw something in the kid. They thought that with the right seasoning, he could develop into an NBA player. Their thinking was that Jeremy could play a season in the NBA's Development League—known as D-League—and see where that took him.

And then Joe Lacob entered the picture.

Who is Joe Lacob?

During the summer of 2010, Lacob was in the midst of purchasing the Golden State Warriors. Even though he had lived in the San Francisco Bay Area for years, he had been part of the Boston Celtics ownership group. When the possibility of purchasing the Golden State Warriors came up, he (along with Peter Guber, the former chairman of Sony Pictures) put together a $450 million tender to buy the team.

So how did this affect Jeremy?

Well, it turns out that Joe Lacob had coached his son's youth basketball team, which played against Jeremy when he was pipsqueak. This fascinating interview between Lacob and *San Jose Mercury News* columnist Tim Kawakami explains things:

Let's just confirm that you made the call to sign Jeremy Lin.

Lacob: It was my call.

Why Lin?

Lacob: Well, that's a special situation.

Your son played with Lin? Against Lin?

Lacob: There were probably three guys that were pretty much the best point guards in high school in this area at that time, and Jeremy Lin was probably the best of them. And my son, Kirk, was right there with him. I've watched them play against each other, and I've coached against him since he was this high.

So I know him from [the time he was] a little kid. Also at Palo Alto I watched him win the state championship over a superior team, and he dominated Mater Dei. And he has heart, he has a lot of talent, he's athletic, which a lot of people don't understand. He's pretty long.

He has a game that translates to the NBA. He can drive,

he's a slasher. He needs to shoot better, obviously. He needs to be a better outside shooter.

It's funny, people don't know his game. They say, oh, he's a shooter but he doesn't have these other skills. No, that's not true, it's the opposite.

Jeremy Lin, I think, can play. He didn't sign because he's Asian-American. That was a nice feature, like anything else. And I think it's great for that community and for the Warriors. But he got signed because he can play.

If you watched his tape, if you watched him in the John Wall thing in Vegas, he played John Wall even up. This is not a guy that shouldn't have been drafted. This is a guy that should've been drafted.

Doesn't that put some pressure on a coach to play him?

Lacob: No, he's got to prove it on the court.

You'll be watching.

Lacob: That's not for me to determine. He has to prove it, coaches have to coach him, and we'll see. Jeremy should've obviously gotten recruited to Stanford. Made a huge error. And by the way, there were a lot of us who were Stanford boosters who were trying to get them to recruit Jeremy. They did not. Well, guess what, that was really stupid. I'm a big Stanford fan, but that was really stupid. The kid was right across the street. You can't recognize that, you've got a problem.

Isn't it great to hear refreshingly plain talk from an NBA owner?

And that's how Jeremy Lin got his chance to play in the NBA. Two weeks after summer league, he signed a two-year contract with the Warriors, and the news of his signing sent a shockwave through the San Francisco Bay Area—especially the Asian-American community. Then, through hustle and grit, he won a spot on the twelve-man roster.

Jeremy made his debut in the Warriors' second game of the 2010–11 season—on "Asian Heritage Night"—before a crowd of 17,408 fans that exploded with cheers when he was inserted into the game with two-and-a-half minutes to go. Jeremy had the honor of dribbling out the final seconds of a hometown victory over the Los Angeles Clippers.

Jeremy Lin had made history. Not only did he become the first Chinese/Taiwanese-American basketball player in the NBA, but he was the first Asian-American to step onto an NBA court. The only other full-blooded American-born Asian to play professional basketball in the United States was 5-foot, 7-inch Wataru "Kilo Wat" Misaka, who played in only *three* games for the New York Knickerbockers back in 1947— in the old Basketball Association of America (BAA), which would become the NBA two years later. Born to Japanese immigrants, Misaka deserves mention for being a pioneer at a time when Americans had just finished defeating Japan in World War II and when memories of Japanese Army atrocities were still fresh in the public's memory.

More importantly, "Kilo Wat," who came along the same year Jackie Robinson broke the color barrier in Major League baseball, was the first non-Caucasian to play professional basketball—a noteworthy achievement since it would be another three years before the NBA admitted its first black player in 1950.

Jeremy's newfound notoriety changed his life. When I spoke with him for *Playing with Purpose*, he said he'd probably been interviewed more than a hundred times in the past year for periodicals ranging from the *New York Times* and *Time* magazine to outlets in Taiwan. Everyone wanted a piece of his time.

His mom and dad, he said, warned him about the temptations found in the NBA. "They said, 'Be smart. There are going to be girls throwing themselves at you, so be smart.' Typical parent stuff. They also reminded me to make sure that I took care of my relationship with God first."

"Do you know that a lot of parents won't say something like that?" I asked.

"I can't imagine my parents *not* saying something," he replied. "That's what makes them awesome."

Another thing Jeremy did before the start of his rookies season was to call probably the most famous Asian-American athlete ever—Michael Chang, who in 1989 became the youngest male to win a Grand Slam tournament when he captured the French Open at the age of seventeen. Chang became a Hall of Fame tennis player who rose to No. 2 in the world during his career.

"I talked with Michael before the season started and asked him about being a Christian in professional sports," Jeremy said. "I picked up some good ideas, like having a consistent devotional time and a prayer team behind you. So I formed a little team that I sent e-mails to every once in a while with prayer requests and praise reports."

"So was it difficult or easy being a Christian in the NBA?" I asked.

"I don't want to say it was easy, but it wasn't as bad as I thought it would be. It helped that I had a couple of teammates who were strong Christians—Stephen Curry and Reggie Williams. We would go to chapel together before the games, and we would occasionally have Christian conversations, so that was definitely helpful. I had a lot of accountability in terms of a small group at home. And I was at home playing for the Warriors, so I went to my home church whenever I could.

"I had my pastor, Stephen Chen, and then I had my small group," Jeremy continued. "And all those things were really helpful. My parents and my family were nearby."

After signing with the Warriors, Jeremy got his own place in Hayward, located roughly midway between his parents' home in Palo Alto and the Oracle Arena in Oakland, where the Warriors play. (His old bedroom in Palo Alto is still adorned with posters of Golden State Warriors players from the past.)

Having his family nearby made the transition into the pros a lot easier, Jeremy said, but the difficult part was not having any type of rhythm.

"You know, church is really tough to attend, and the schedule is so crazy. I had to listen to sermons on my computer on a lot of Sundays. The sermons would not always be from my home church but from a variety of places. My dad burned a bunch of sermons for me onto a CD, so I would carry a little case of all the sermons. Devotionals were a big part of my walk this year—just quiet times in my hotel rooms."

I asked Jeremy about those stretches in hotel rooms since there's a lot of downtime in the NBA during long road trips that can stretch from five to eight days.

"Yeah, I had more spare time this year and more time

to spend with God this year than I have ever had," he said. "That was one of the parts that made it easier versus in college, where you wake up, go to class, practice, then do your homework and go to sleep. I had a lot more free time since I was no longer in school."

"And what about the temptations?" I asked. "I imagine one of the difficulties about playing in the NBA is all the women hanging around the hotel rooms and all the people trying to talk to you and that type of thing."

"Yes, I think that's definitely true, but it wasn't really an issue for me because I didn't go out very much. And then there were guys on my team that I hung out with, and we had a different lifestyle, so it wasn't a huge issue. But it's definitely out there if you want it, but I chose to take it out of play. Once you take a stand for something at the beginning, everybody respects that and they don't bother you about it."

I asked Jeremy what he thought about attending a chapel service with players from the other team—players he would later try to beat on the basketball floor—one hour before game time.

"I was surprised, but it was really cool to see believers from other teams. Actually, I enjoyed that a lot. There were more believers, more people attending chapel, than I would have thought playing in the NBA. Before the season started, people warned me about this or about that with NBA players, kind of lumped them into one big category, one big stereotype, but I didn't find this to be the case at all. I also think my first year in the league broke a lot of stereotypes."

Jeremy wears No. 7—the biblical number that denotes completeness or perfection—and local fans loved cheering for their native son. But all the attention created an intense spotlight that followed him everywhere, and it became apparent that he was and would be a work in progress as a basketball player.

In late December 2010, the Warriors reassigned Jeremy—who had been averaging seventeen minutes a game—to their D-League affiliate, the Reno Bighorns. It was hard for him not to see the move as a demotion.

"It was a shock because I did not realize how different the two leagues were," he said. "It was also humbling because the locker rooms, facilities, attendance at games, the travel—it was all very different. Playing in Reno gave me a whole new perspective on everything. In the NBA, it was easy to complain about this or about that, but after being in D-League, I gained a greater sense of gratitude."

The Warriors coaching staff sent him down to give him playing time, and for the rest of the season, he bounced back and forth between Reno and Oakland. By the end of his rookie season, he had played in twenty-nine NBA games, averaging ten minutes a game for a struggling Golden State team that finished 36–46.

So how did he take all those difficulties?

"It was really hard," he confessed. "People don't believe me when I say my rookie season was the toughest year of my life, but it was. I had a lot of long nights and struggles. I had to really learn how to submit my will to God and learn to trust Him while going through different situations that I thought were maybe unfair at times or things that I had wished would have gone in a different way.

"What I learned was to lean on God in those situations,

and to make my relationship more intimate by spending more time with Him every day. I did a lot of reading and I did a lot of praying. More praying than I had ever done. I just learned a ton."

Don't you just love his attitude?

That attitude, as well as his will and determination, is why Jeremy is a player you want to keep an eye on.

Because he's playing with purpose.

6

LUKE RIDNOUR:
HEIR TO PISTOL PETE

Luke Ridnour was in fourth grade when his schoolteacher announced a big assignment she wanted Luke and his classmates to complete in two weeks.

The task?

Write a three-page paper on a person of their choosing.

Luke shifted eagerly in his seat. He knew exactly whom he wanted to write about.

When school let out, Luke gathered his backpack and sprinted from the rear of Blaine Primary School, past the green tennis courts, to the Blaine High gymnasium. The elementary school, middle school, and high school were located on the same campus, so the distance was only a hundred yards. Luke knew his father—a PE teacher and the high school's head basketball coach—would be in his office preparing for practice.

The Ridnour family lived in Blaine, Washington, a small town of four thousand situated in the very northwest corner of the continental United States. The border town is the terminus point for Interstate 5, the West Coast highway that links the Canadian border with the boundary of Mexico, 1,381 miles to the south. Blaine's colorful past dates back to the Fraser River gold rush of 1858, which brought an influx of eager prospectors into the region.

When Luke bounced into Rob Ridnour's office that afternoon, he told his dad about the assignment he had received that day.

"Who are you going to write about?" his father asked.

"Pistol Pete."

Of course, Rob thought.

Ten-year-old Luke knew about Pistol Pete because he and the family had recently watched *The Pistol: The Birth of a Legend*, a video that had been released a few months earlier. The slice-of-life movie told the story about Pete Maravich's eighth-grade year when he played on the varsity basketball team at Daniel High School in Central, South Carolina, despite being too young to attend the school.

Set in 1961, the film recounted how Pete's teammates ostracized him because of his young age and because of his unworldly talent for shooting and whipping behind-the-back passes. *The Pistol* also explored the supportive father-son relationship between Pete and his father, Press Maravich, who was a former pro player and Clemson University coach.

"Well, you'll have to do some research on Pistol Pete before you write your paper," said Luke's father, who knew the entire Maravich story. Rob was a middle-schooler in the late

1960s when Pete's sleight-of-hand artistry left crowds gasping and sportswriters crooning about the new sensation from Louisiana State University. (You'll read a lot more about Pete Maravich in the last chapter.)

Over the next couple weeks, Luke read Maravich's autobiography, *Heir to a Dream,* and also watched *Pistol Pete's Homework Basketball* training videos, which mesmerized him. Luke had been dribbling a basketball since age three and was a very skilled player for his age, but Pete could make the basketball do things he'd never seen before. Pete's effortless demonstration of ball-handling prowess captivated Luke's young imagination.

Luke emulated everything Pistol Pete did on the *Homework Basketball* videos—from ball-handling exercises like the Square V dribble, the crossover dribble, and the through-the-legs dribble, to positioning his wrist properly so as to impart backspin and thus more control on the jump shot. Luke even taught himself to twirl the ball on his right index finger like a spinning top.

Since Pete had said he took a basketball everywhere with him when he was a youngster, Luke started doing the same thing. He started carrying a basketball into Blaine Primary School and dribbling in the hallway on his way to class, though he sometimes got into trouble for being disruptive. After the final bell, he would dribble from the elementary school to his father's office inside the gym, where he'd hang out for a bit before leaving to shoot baskets with the high school players.

"I emulated everything I saw Pete do because I wanted to handle the basketball just like he did," Luke said. "I tried dribbling from a car while my dad drove down the street, and I dribbled on a railroad rail, but that was pretty difficult."

Luke even slept with his basketball, just like Pete.

There was another reason Rob Ridnour and his wife, Muriel, supported Luke's desire to write a paper on Pete Maravich. You see, Pistol was very outspoken about the transformation he had experienced after accepting Jesus Christ as his Lord and Savior following his retirement from pro basketball. That part of Pete's story was the focal point of *Heir to a Dream*, which was published a few months prior to his death from a sudden heart attack at age forty.

Rob and Muriel had Luke listen to a "Focus on the Family" broadcast in which Dr. James Dobson talked about the dramatic morning when Maravich collapsed and died after playing in a pickup basketball game with the Focus on the Family radio host and members of his staff. "I learned that Pistol Pete, toward the end of his life, was sold out for Jesus," Luke said. "That was the big thing that stands out in my memory, more than the basketball stuff. Yes, Pete was passionate about basketball, but when he found Jesus, that became his main passion."

Luke's parents were familiar with Dr. Dobson because they listened to Christian radio programs like "Focus on the Family" on Praise 106.5 FM while riding in the car. In addition, they raised Luke and his older sister, Heather, in the Christian faith and took them to church every Sunday morning and Wednesday night.

A COMMITMENT TO THE GAME
While working on his Pistol Pete paper, Luke saw the commitment Pete had made to the game at a young age—and he

was inspired to do the same. Beginning in the fifth grade, he would get up at five every morning, rain or shine, to start his training regimen.

Blaine, since it lies so far north, can be a chilly, damp place in winter. The average highs in December and January are barely above 40 degrees, and it's not unusual for the lows to dip into the 20s. Rain is a constant. That never stopped Luke from his workouts, though. "He would religiously get up and do those drills *every* morning," Rob said. "Rain, snow . . . it didn't matter. He was out there every day from the fifth grade through his senior year of high school, even in winter and the pre-dawn darkness."

One Saturday, Luke had set a goal of making fifteen hundred free throws. Even though there was a driving snow storm in Blaine that day, Luke stayed outside, his numb fingers stiff from the freezing cold, until he made his fifteen hundred free throws.

Rob had installed a basketball rim in the backyard patio, and that's where Luke practiced every morning before school. He began his training with a jump rope routine to warm up, and then he'd move into the "Maravich drills" he'd seen in the videos or that his father used in his summer basketball camps.

On one occasion, Luke asked his father how he could increase his quickness. "Now we're talking about a fifth-grader asking that question, which shows you how determined he was to improve every facet of his game," Rob said. "I told him boxers always had good body balance, good footwork, and improved quickness from jumping rope. So he decided to try rope jumping, and Luke became very good at it. I think jumping all that rope really helped his career. He's always had good feet and good body balance."

All that hard work—day after day, week after week—helped Luke make big leaps in his game. While he was still in elementary school, he would get the local parents clapping and cheering at his father's games at Blaine High when he put on dribbling demonstrations during halftime. Luke, whose specialty was simultaneously dribbling two balls at the same time, could dribble circles around anyone.

After seeing his halftime shows, friends of Luke's parents lavished praise on him, and some started calling him "Cool Hand Luke"—after the famous 1960s film starring Paul Newman.

By the sixth grade, Luke had outgrown his middle school competition in Whatcom County, so his parents had him try out for an elite travel team from Seattle. When he was accepted, it necessitated some huge sacrifices on his parents' part. They had to drive Luke 220 miles round-trip to the big city three times a week for practices and games.

COURT HUSTLER

When Luke Ridnour was in middle school, he'd often challenge the high school players on his father's team to three-point shooting contests before they started practice. The stakes: a bottle of Gatorade from the vending machine.

It wasn't long before the upperclassmen discovered that shooting treys against Luke was a losing bet.

So one time Luke said he'd shoot his three-pointers left-handed. This time he got some takers.

Big mistake.

They all had to pay up.

Luke was one of the youngest kids on the Seattle travel team—and the only white player. His black teammates called him "Casper," but that didn't bother Luke—in fact, he had fun with it. His team played in numerous AAU tournaments up and down the West Coast, which necessitated expensive road trips but also boosted Luke's basketball experience and abilities. His Central Area Youth Association (CAYA) team qualified for a national tournament in Lexington, Kentucky, and played in Florida.

All that tournament experience helped Luke make great strides in his game, and that was a big help when he started playing for his father during his freshman year of high school. Luke would become a dominant high school player and would help guide the Blaine Borderites (don't you love that mascot name?) to the Washington Class 2A state championship during his junior season. The grateful townspeople threw a huge parade down H Street for their favorite son and favorite team.

As Luke headed into his senior year, everyone could see that the 6-foot, 2-inch point guard was an awesome talent. All the 5:00 a.m. workouts, all the after-dinner shooting in the Blaine High gym, and all the out-of-state competition paid off as college scholarship offers began rolling in. College coaches could see he was a natural in the way he created separation with the dribble, pumped the perfect pass to his teammates, displayed his silky stroke at the free-throw line, and showed leadership on the floor.

Luke was the prototypical point guard the top-flight college basketball programs desired. Kentucky and Utah wanted him. So did Gonzaga University, an up-and-coming program in Spokane, located in the eastern part of Washington. In the Pac-10, the University of Washington was waiting to roll out the purple carpet in Seattle. Further south, Oregon and Oregon State both wanted Luke, but he couldn't visit both schools because he only had one recruiting trip left. The NCAA limits high school players to five out-of-town recruiting trips.

Luke flipped a coin to see which Oregon school he would visit. The University of Oregon won, and during his weekend visit in Eugene, he called his parents to tell him how much fun he was having.

Luke liked what he saw during his recruiting trip. I'm sure McArthur Court—the field house known as "The Pit" because of the way the crazy fans sit in bleachers almost directly on top of the players and shake the building from its wooden rafters to its hardwood floor—made a huge impression on him. Built in 1926, Mac Court's electric atmosphere was the consummate stage for college basketball.

Luke committed to Oregon before the start of his senior year, but he didn't put his game into cruise control. The way he played during his final season made him the talk of high school basketball in the state of Washington. Luke and his teammates at Blaine High netted another state championship, and McDonald's and *Parade* magazine named Luke a high school All-American.

During his four seasons of high school varsity basketball, Luke led the Blaine Borderites to a 97–11 record.

GO, DUCKS, GO!

Eugene, Oregon's second-largest city, is a college town, pure and simple. Humorist Dave Barry once said that Eugene is "approximately 278 billion miles from anything," but that's not really true. Eugene is a happening place—and the birthplace of Nike—that evokes a retro vibe that comes from a high concentration of hippies and vegetarian restaurants. While the Emerald City promotes its natural beauty and recreational opportunities—with a focus on the arts, alternative lifestyles, and a live-and-let-live culture—at the end of the day, Eugene is a small city that revolves around the twenty-three thousand students attending the University of Oregon.

Sure, Eugene is also a liberal enclave, where protests against "Big Oil" are clothing optional and people pass the tofu pâté around a campfire of hemp. But once you get beyond the red flannel shirts and the Birkenstocks, people are people. Not many are Christians, though. Eugene is the least-churched city in the least-churched state in the country. No one would ever confuse the Willamette Valley with the Bible Belt.

Yet Luke will tell you that it was a divine appointment for him to play his college career in Eugene for the Oregon Ducks, and much of the reason is because he met an ex-marine who mentored him during this three-year career at the school.

That ex-marine was Keith Jenkins, pastor of Jubilee World Outreach Church, which grew from a congregation of seventeen persons in 1996 to nearly a thousand while Luke was in Eugene.

"Pastor Keith," as the Oregon athletes called him, was a volunteer chaplain for the University of Oregon sports teams who forged deep bonds with Duck athletes. In Luke, Pastor Keith saw a young man from the uppermost corner of Washington who needed a place of refuge, a Christian community he could plug into.

It helped that Luke's coach at Oregon, Ernie Kent, encouraged his players to foster relationships with their team chaplain. Luke didn't have to be asked twice. He and Pastor Keith met for Bible studies, and those times of reading God's Word deepened Luke's faith immeasurably. Sure, he had believed in Jesus since he started playing biddy basketball, but the things Pastor Keith taught him about God kicked things up a notch. "Really, when I started reading the Word with my chaplain, everything changed—the way I thought, the way I acted, and my attitude," Luke said. "It was like I was being washed by the Word."

Luke had a frustrating freshman year at Oregon, averaging 7 points a game and shooting 33 percent from the field for a Duck team that was expected to do better. Oregon won half its games, finishing 14–14, but posted a dismal 5–13 record in the Pac-10 Conference. Still, Luke attracted notice for his play and was voted to the Pac-10 All-Freshman team.

Luke, who wanted to have a better sophomore year, went back to work during the off-season. It was hard to keep him out of Mac Court. Thanks to his father, Luke was used to having his own key to the gym, but at Mac Court, he had to be more creative. He made his way in during off hours by sticking athletic tape over the strike plate of one of the broad doors leading to the locker room so it wouldn't lock.

During Luke's sophomore season, the Duck basketball program won a lot of games because of him and *another* Luke on the team—Luke Jackson, a left-handed 6-foot, 7-inch small forward with a sweet jump shot and athletic in-the-paint moves. The two collaborated on a rip-and-run style that often saw Luke Ridnour accept an outlet pass, run the floor on the fast break, and hit the streaking Luke Jackson for a lay-in or dunk. Coach Ernie Kent preached up-tempo basketball—the equivalent of a no-huddle, two-minute offense in football—and that was the two Lukes' kind of game. Defenses chased Luke & Luke all game long.

As the Ducks piled up wins during the 2001–02 season, sportswriters began proclaiming Luke Ridnour the best point guard in the country—someone who could play in the NBA. Glowing stories about Luke called him an "old school" player who could have stepped off the set of the movie *Hoosiers*, the 1986 film about a small-town Indiana high school basketball team that won the state championship in 1952, at a time when all high schools in Indiana, regardless of size, competed in one state championship tournament. Sportswriters compared him to Jimmy Chitwood, the shy, reserved player who made the last-second shot to win the title for Hickory High.

Luke also showed spiritual leadership on a team that included a half-dozen Christians—including Luke Jackson—by helping organize voluntary pregame chapels and by asking the entire team to recite the Lord's Prayer in the locker room before tipoff. These "kumbaya" moments translated to the court, too: the Ducks were ranked in the top five in the country for eleven different offensive categories during the 2001–02 season, including No. 1 in points per possession and true shooting percentage.

These Ducks liked to pass the ball around, and most of the assists came from Luke Ridnour, who showed an uncanny ability to penetrate and dish as well as work the pick-and-roll with his teammate and friend, Luke Jackson. Coach Kent summed up his point guard's contribution this way:

"He gives himself up for his teammates."

The Luke & Luke Show helped the Ducks capture their first Pac-10 championship since 1945 and advance to the Elite Eight in the NCAA Tournament. Their title dreams ended with a loss to the No. 1 overall seed Kansas, however.

Back to sneaking into Mac Court through one of the taped-up back doors during the off-season.

ONE MORE COLLEGE SEASON . . .
THEN ON TO THE NBA

The fall before his junior year at Oregon, Luke was named to *Playboy* magazine's preseason All-American team. As far as Luke was concerned, however, that was a non-starter. He politely turned down *Playboy*, saying, "My mom wouldn't be too happy about it, and I didn't feel I should do it. It's a great accomplishment and all that, but it was a beliefs thing for me."

Interesting how God honored that stand. Not too long after Luke passed on *Playboy*, Nike announced it was commissioning a 50-by-170-foot billboard of Luke as a candidate for the Wooden Award, one of college basketball's top individual honors. The seventeen-story portrait of Luke, with ball on hip, was erected on a skyscraper near New York City's Times Square.

Luke didn't win the Wooden Award during his junior year at Oregon, but he cemented his status as one of the elite players in college basketball. He won plenty of other awards, including Pac-10 Conference Player of the Year after averaging 19.7 points a game.

The iron was hot, and it was time to strike and turn pro, although the Mac Court fans chanted "One more year!" so loudly during Luke's last home game that play had to be stopped as he walked off the court.

Luke made himself available for the 2003 NBA draft, and lo and behold, his hometown team, the Seattle SuperSonics, took him as the fourteenth pick. It many ways, it was a dream come true for Luke and his family: he would be playing NBA basketball within driving distance of his hometown of Blaine, meaning his parents could come to a lot of his games. Also, the Sonics needed a talented point guard prospect to replace aging Gary Payton, who was traded to Milwaukee.

Prior to his rookie season, Luke underwent surgery on his abdomen and groin, which forced him to miss nearly the entire slate of preseason games. Once he was healthy, he played in spurts—sometimes ten minutes a night, sometime twenty-five. His rookie season was marked by ups and downs, which were reflected in the team's season. Seattle floundered and missed the playoffs with a 37–45 record.

Luke had a breakout season during his second year in the league. He won a starting position in training camp, and with Luke quarterbacking the offense from his point-guard position and sharpshooter Ray Allen scoring from the shooting guard slot, the Sonics turned things around. Seattle was the surprise of the NBA early in the 2004–05 season, winning 23 of its first 29 games. The Sonics climbed to the heady heights of 40–16 in early March before slumping the last six weeks of the season. After finishing 52–30, their quest for a championship was dashed with a loss to the San Antonio Spurs in the second round of the NBA playoffs.

SETTLING IN AND SETTLING DOWN

Luke's sophomore season showed that he belonged in the NBA, and since then, he has settled into a good pro basketball career. Off the court, he also decided to settle down, too. In August 2005, he married Kate Reome, whom he had been dating for three years.

Luke and Kate first met during the state basketball tournament in his senior year of high school. They had both been asked to appear at a Rotary Club luncheon honoring the best high school basketball players in the state. Luke represented Blaine High, while Kate was invited on behalf of Lakeside High in Spokane.

Luke and Kate sat next to each other at the luncheon. Kate knew about Luke because all the girls on her team had a crush on this cute boy with tight blond curls. Kate wasn't completely impressed, though, because she thought Luke looked like a slacker. He was dressed in his standard uniform—faded T-shirt, beige cargo shorts, and backwards hat—while everyone else, including herself, had dressed nicely for the occasion.

Luke went off to the University of Oregon, while Kate had another year of high school before moving on to Central Washington University in Ellensburg, where she had earned a scholarship to play volleyball. You would think that would be the last time Luke and Kate would ever see each other. But you'd be wrong.

Luke and Kate's opportunity to "reconnect" started when she visited a guy friend who happened to be an acquaintance of the Ridnours. She needed to get this fellow's e-mail address— as well as the e-mails of any of their common friends—because she had lost her contact list.

As her friend scrolled through his smartphone, his voice raised an octave. "Oh, here's Luke's e-mail! Do you remember him?"

Sure, she remembered Luke Ridnour. He was practically famous in Washington sports circles. But she didn't think it was a good idea to send Luke a "Hi, howya doing?" e-mail out of the blue; after all, it had been two years since their one meeting at the Rotary luncheon. She thought that if she e-mailed him, he'd probably think she was some eighth-grade teenybopper.

Kate changed her mind, though, and sent Luke a friendly e-mail reminding him of how they sat at the same table at the Rotary luncheon. The e-mail went out during March Madness in 2002, the year the Ducks were in the national championship hunt.

To her everlasting surprise, Luke quickly responded and said, "Of course, I remember you."

As they got to know each other through phone calls and e-mail messages, Luke learned that he and Kate were in sync spiritually. Back in high school, she had become interested in Christianity while attending Young Life events. Then several of her girlfriends invited her to a Wednesday night service. That night, the speaker said if anyone at the service hadn't made a decision to accept Jesus into their life, now would be a great time to do it. Kate knew she didn't understand everything about Christianity, but something in her heart prompted her to move forward and start down the road of life . . . with Jesus Christ holding her hand every step of the way.

Luke and Kate's long-distance relationship grew slowly. After three years, their love blossomed. When she walked down the aisle in a wedding dress, on the arm of her father, she was ready to marry a young man she was crazy in love with.

Here's how Kate described her courtship to Jill Ewert, editor of *Sharing the Victory* magazine:

You must have made a big impression on him then.

Kate Ridnour: You know, I guess so. He told me later on that after we met at that Rotary Club, he went home and tried to get my phone number from my high school. I kidded him that he was a stalker.

But I look back on that day when I went over to my friend's place to get those e-mail addresses. It was such a God thing because it was windy out. I was like, *I don't want to go anywhere.* But then I decided to go see this guy so that I could keep in touch with friends. Funny how things panned out.

You can see how you almost didn't go, right?

Kate: Oh, yeah! Looking back you can see how it was just scripted, you know? God was like, *Okay, go here. Go there. Okay, e-mail. Talk. Now you're together.*

It's funny. It's almost a boring story because we weren't high school sweethearts. But it's neat because I did know him before he was in the league. I knew him before he was the big Luke Ridnour from the Seattle SuperSonics. I knew the little, scrawny white guy.

Is that how you still think about him?

Kate: Oh, no! He's so much bigger. He's strong and manly! But you know, he is just a boy. There are things that he does and in how he acts. He's just a boy in a big man's world.

Believe me, Kate was not in any way putting down her husband. For the longest time, Luke was content to drive around an old beat-up truck, but his sensible wife pointed out to him that he was being pennywise but pound foolish—if the truck broke down when he was on his way to practice and he was late, the fine would be five thousand dollars.

The couple lived in a waterfront home on Lake Washington that Luke had purchased after the Sonics drafted him. Following their marriage, they settled into the NBA lifestyle—but not the lifestyle many associate with professional basketball players. Luke was a devoted husband who had no interest in straying. Being separated from Kate during long road trips wasn't easy for him, so Luke took advantage of advances in modern technology. He and Kate got into Skype, a software application that allows users to make voice calls over the Internet and to see each other via webcams on their computers. As soon as he arrived at the team hotel—as long as it wasn't late at night or in the wee hours—Luke would call his wife for a chat.

I asked Luke how he handled it when the team bus pulled up to the player hotel at 3:00 a.m., following a plane flight, and he saw all sorts of women hanging out in the lobby. Since he always walked straight to his room without passing Go or collecting two hundred dollars, as they say, how did he protect himself from temptation?

By wearing the full armor of God, he told me.

Luke says that Ephesians 6:11—"Put on the full armor of God, so that you can take your stand against the devil's schemes"—is a reminder that Satan will always try to come at him but that the Lord always prevails in the lives of those who "armor up."

BENDS IN THE ROAD

Three years into their marriage, life threw Luke and Kate a pair of curves—on the same day. They weren't *bad* curves . . . just new bends in the road for them to navigate.

The 2007–08 season, Luke's fifth in the league, was filled with turmoil for the SuperSonics. The team had been sold in 2006 to a group of investors from Oklahoma City that included Clay Bennett. The handwriting was on the wall: Bennett threatened to move the team to Oklahoma if a deal for a new lease at KeyArena couldn't be worked out between the franchise and the city of Seattle. The Sonics were looking like a lame duck team to their fans.

Then, in August 2008, a blockbuster trade involving three teams and six players was announced, and it included Luke, who was being shipped to the Milwaukee Bucks.

Trades happen in the NBA.

On the same day, Luke heard that he would be playing for Milwaukee, he and Kate learned she was pregnant with their first child. That was a double-barrel blast of family news.

Kate always liked the name Trey, but after Luke got *traded*, she started playing around with that verb and came up with "Tradon"—pronounced TRAY-don.

"I think it's a pretty unique name," Luke said.

Tradon Lukas Ridnour was born on April 13, 2009.

Luke played two seasons with the Bucks, averaging 10.9 points, 4.9 assists, and 2.2 rebounds per game. He became a free agent after the 2009–10 season and signed a four-year, $16 million contract with the Minnesota Timberwolves.

Luke's veteran presence on the floor was an asset, but the T-wolves fell on hard times during the 2010–11 season, compiling the NBA's worst record at 17–65. As the losses piled up like snowdrifts, Kate learned she was expecting again. Ultrasounds revealed that the Ridnours would become parents of twin boys in early February 2011.

When Beckett and Kyson Ridnour were born, Luke and Kate were stunned to learn that Kyson suffered from life-threatening complications in the esophageal area. Though Kyson's condition has made for difficult times in the Ridnour household, Luke and Kate hold fast to their faith in God.

And they're praying for a miracle.

"I don't want to get into the details of what's going on, but Kate and I believe that one day there will be an amazing testimony that we'll be able to share with thousands and thousands of people about the miracle that God has done," Luke said.

Luke and Kate have received emotional support from friends and from the pastor of their home church in Seattle, who flew into Minneapolis to pray and lay hands on Kyson. (The Ridnours maintain a permanent home near Seattle during the off-season.) Their home church, Eastridge Church in Issaquah, sent out prayer chain updates regarding the family's difficult situation.

"It's been a tough go for the family," said Rob, "an emotional time for Luke, but he's holding on to his faith and praying for God's healing."

It hasn't been easy, but Luke says he has an extreme amount of peace about what will happen with Kyson as the family perseveres through this tough time.

"We believe miracles still happen."

7

THEY'RE PLAYING
WITH PURPOSE, TOO

Here's an interesting starting five to take the floor for an NBA game: Luke Ridnour and Jeremy Lin at guard, Anthony Parker and Kyle Korver at forward, and Chris Kaman at center.

But as Ernie Johnson pointed out in this book's foreword, there are other NBA players trying to live out their faith as well as play great basketball for their teams. Here are a half-dozen other players—as well as an NBA chaplain, coach, and general manager to watch out for:

STEPHEN CURRY
GOLDEN STATE WARRIORS
Twenty-three-year-old Stephen Curry has some impressive genes working for him.

Stephen, the son of former NBA sharpshooter Dell Curry and former Virginia Tech volleyball standout Sonya Curry, is coming off a strong second season with the Golden State Warriors. As the team's point guard, he averaged 18.6 points and 5.8 assists in thirty-four minutes a game during the 2010–11 season—although it remains to be seen how much of a load he will carry in the upcoming year.

Stephen became a Christian in fifth grade when he responded to an altar call at Central Church of God in Charlotte, North Carolina. His parents thought it was important that he attend a Christian high school, so he played prep ball at Charlotte Christian School, where he scored more than 1,400 points to become the school's all-time leading scorer.

Stephen's father played for Virginia Tech back in the day, so he naturally wanted to follow in his father's footsteps. But when the Hokies didn't offer him a scholarship, he chose a school close to home—Davidson College in Davidson, North Carolina—that played a Division I schedule and occasionally qualified to play in the NCAA tournament.

One time before a preseason practice heading into his freshman season at Davidson, Stephen opened a cardboard box containing a new pair of sneakers. He then took a Sharpie pen with silver ink and wrote "Romans 8:28" on each toe as a reminder of his mother's favorite verse. That became something he did with all his basketball shoes.

It was during Stephen's sophomore year at Davidson that he first attracted national attention. During the 2008 NCAA tournament, he led tiny Davidson all the way to the Elite Eight. The Wildcats registered upset victories over Gonzaga, Georgetown, and Wisconsin before the Kansas Jayhawks, the eventual national champions, ended their Cinderella run with a 58–57 win in front of seventy thousand fans at Ford Field in Detroit.

During the 2008 March Madness tournament, Stephen averaged 34 points a game (including 30 in the *second half* against Gonzaga), prompting reporters to ask him about the meaning behind a different silver inscription on his sneakers that read: "I can do all things." Was he exhibiting the "look at me" mentality that's often seen today, or was it a simple case of an overblown ego?

"Oh, that," Stephen replied. "That's Philippians 4:13: 'I can do all things through him who strengthens me,'" he told reporters. "It's always been one of my favorite Bible verses [because it helps me] realize that what I do on the floor isn't a measure of my own strength. Having that there keeps me focused on the game, a constant reminder of who I'm playing for."

Stephen upped his scoring production during his junior year to 28.6 points per game—the best in the nation. As a consensus All-American getting a lot of ink, he decided to skip his senior season and turn pro. The Golden State Warriors took him with the seventh pick in the first round of the 2009 NBA draft.

Stephen had a good rookie season in 2009–10, and he finished second in the Rookie of the Year voting. He then backed up his solid first year with an outstanding second season with the Warriors. His future is bright as he plays to bring glory to God through basketball.

Keep an eye on Stephen, just like his headmaster at Charlotte Christian School, Dr. Leo Orsino, has been doing for the last half-dozen years. It turns out that Dr. Orsino is a blogger, and he had this to say about his former student:

> *On behalf of the faculty, staff, and Board of Trustees, we want to congratulate Stephen Curry and his family. We are extremely proud of him and blessed by his character and accomplishments.*
>
> *Can you imagine being on national television? Can you imagine handling all of the pressure both on and off the court? Everyone who knows Stephen is not surprised by his success of Christ-honoring character. We experienced the same "humble superstar spirit" both on and off the court while he was a student at Charlotte Christian School. There is no doubt that there is something very special about Stephen Curry. We already know what makes him special. He loves Jesus Christ and knows the Truth of God.*

NENÊ
DENVER NUGGETS

Nenê (the circumflex is often dropped in favor of an un-accented *e* when printed in the United States) is the legal name of Maybyner Rodney Hilário, the power forward/center for the Denver Nuggets.

Nenê, a native of Brazil, is the latest in a long line of Brazilian sports stars who have changed their legal names to a single word. Think Pelé, Ronaldo, Kaká, and Ronaldinho.

These one-word names have cropped up over the years because Brazilian full names tend to be rather long (for example, Pelé, the great soccer star of the 1960s and '70s, was christened Edson Arantes do Nascimento, which is a handful to pronounce). But the greater reason is because Brazilians value individuality and flair on the field, so going to a one-word moniker fosters a more intimate, romantic relationship with the fans. And probably more media attention as well, which is the name of the game when it comes to "branding" yourself and getting endorsement deals.

Enter Nenê, a 6-foot, 11-inch, 250-pound powerhouse with the Denver Nuggets since the 2002–03 season. Such a massive man taking the name Nenê—which means *baby* in Portuguese, the official language of Brazil—is filled with irony. Nenê is the only player in the NBA to go with only one name, and that makes him truly unique among professional basketball players.

Nenê's a late bloomer in the game of basketball. After playing soccer for most of his childhood and learning that sport was probably not in his future professionally, he took up basketball at the relatively late age of fourteen. He improved quickly, though, and turned pro at age sixteen, playing for a Brazilian team known as Vasco da Gama. He got his big break after an NBA pre-draft camp in 2002, when the New York Knicks drafted him but promptly traded him to Denver.

Moving to the United States at the age of nineteen presented challenges for Nenê. Not only did he have a lot to learn about playing in the NBA, but he also had to learn a new language, adjust to the different foods here in the States (no *frango com quiabo,* or chicken with okra), and live in a cold city (the Mile High city of Denver). He has adapted well, and he now speaks fantastic English and connects with fans. On the court, he has performed admirably for the Nuggets, showing that he is a player who can dominate the offensive end of the court. His critics, however, say he lacks aggression and is soft on defense.

Nenê said he is seriously thinking of retiring by 2016 to work in ministry at his church in Brazil, known as God Is the Answer.

"I have like a deal for my pastor," he told one interviewer. "I want to get involved with the church right here in Brazil. If my financial situation is stable, why am I going to [want to] have more money? I'm not crazy for money. I think the best I can do is with the church . . . I can help with things with my testimony."

Nenê will be thirty-three at the start of the 2015–16 season, and athletes are notorious for changing their minds about retirement (and who can blame them since jobs that pay several million dollars—even tens of millions of dollars—come to few individuals who inhabit this planet). But Nenê has shown that his heart is in the right place as he looks at his future beyond the boundaries of the basketball court.

Perhaps facing his mortality several years ago helped him see things in a different light.

In early 2008, Nenê took a leave of absence from the Nuggets after he learned why he hadn't been feeling well: at the age of twenty-four, he had testicular cancer. Several other high-profile athletes have dealt with this serious, life-threatening disease, including bicyclist Lance Armstrong, ice skater Scott Hamilton, and baseball player/ESPN commentator John Kruk.

In January 2008, Nenê submitted to surgery to have his right testicle and a malignant tumor removed. "It was scary, but I believe in God," Nenê told the *Denver Post* when he went public with his story in the spring of 2008. "And now I'm a survivor."

So far, it looks like Nenê's doctors detected and treated the cancer early enough. And with the departure of Carmelo Anthony to the New York Knicks during the 2010–11 season, the Denver Nuggets are looking to Nenê to hold down the fort until a better cast is assembled around him.

But the Denver front office had better work quickly.

There's a church in Brazil waiting for Nenê to arrive and lend a hand in ministry.

REGGIE WILLIAMS
GOLDEN STATE WARRIORS

You'd think that leading the NCAA in scoring for two consecutive seasons would make a player a lock to play in the NBA.

But things didn't happen that way for Reggie Williams, the shooting guard from Virginia Military Institute (or VMI) who quarterbacked a run-and-gun offense that regularly scored more than 100 points per game—not an easy task in a forty-minute game.

When Reggie wasn't selected in the 2008 NBA draft, he kept a great attitude. He didn't lash out in anger or complain but said that being passed over "definitely made me humble myself." Sure that God had a different plan for his life, Reggie took his game overseas—like Anthony Parker did—and played for a French team in Dijon, France.

Reggie put enough *moutarde* on his jump shot in Dijon to earn a spot the following season with the Sioux Falls Skyforce of the NBA Development League—the Triple A level of professional basketball. This was actually something of a step back for Reggie. He didn't have a car in frigid South Dakota and was paid a scant $19,000 for the season, but the way he saw it, playing in Sioux Falls was his best chance to get a shot in the NBA. He played great in Sioux Falls and, finally, the phone rang. The Golden State Warriors were on the line, and they offered Reggie a ten-day "take-a-look" contract toward the end of the 2009–10 season.

Reggie showed enough moxie and game that Golden State signed him for the 2010–11 season. Reggie joined Jeremy Lin as another rookie guard trying to make an impression with the Warriors. He also got a salary bump to $762,195 for the season.

Even though he and Jeremy came from different backgrounds and college experiences, they were brothers in Christ. The pair fell in with each other for morale and support.

In Reggie's first outing of the 2010–11 season, he turned a few heads when he scored 10 points, dished out five assists, and grabbed five rebounds in twenty minutes of playing time against the Miami Heat, who would later lose to the Dallas Mavericks in the 2011 NBA Finals.

Reggie had a knack for making buckets, whether he was taking awkward but athletic shots ten to fifteen feet from the basket, or drilling spot-up jumpers from beyond the three-point line. He found ways to score within the flow of the game, showing that he's the type of player who can "quietly" score 20 points in a game.

Reggie didn't receive consistent minutes during his rookie season, so his stats were up and down. But he nailed his three-point shots with Korver-like accuracy, making 42 percent of his tries beyond the arc. He scored more than 20 points in five games, but there also plenty of games in which he scored just 2 or 3 points.

Finally, we have this anecdote to share about Reggie:

When Reggie mentioned to the media that he was looking for a church to attend, Pastor Ryan Nash of Union Baptist Church in nearby Oakland went to a Facebook page dedicated to Reggie (but not Reggie's personal page) to invite him to drop by. "Please feel free to come by anytime, no pressure to join," the pastor wrote. "I just want to offer a place where you could worship. Please forgive this form of communication as I had no other way to reach you."

When Reggie put himself out there and told reporters

covering the Warriors that he was looking for a church, he sent a signal about who he was and what was important to him.

And that's cool to see from an NBA player.

NICK COLLISON
OKLAHOMA CITY THUNDER

Maybe Nick Collison should change his name to Nick *Collision*.

The 6-foot, 10-inch power forward with the Oklahoma City Thunder is known for planting his feet in the lane and letting the LeBrons and the Carmelos of the league plow into him so that he can draw the offensive foul.

It's called "taking a charge."

Charges taken is not an official NBA statistic, but if it were, Nick would probably rank among the league leaders. What he does is the spiritual equivalent of giving his body up for his teammates—something the apostle Paul wrote about: "No, I strike a blow to my body and make it my slave so that after I have preached to others, I myself will not be disqualified for the prize" (1 Corinthians 9:27).

Here's how Nick "strikes a blow" to his body. When a bulky and well-built behemoth charges toward the rim—only to find Nick blocking his path—what happens next isn't pretty. The crash usually sends both players to the floor—and it's almost always Nick who gets the worst of it. Even a collision with a diminutive point guard can hurt since he's coming at full speed and often sticks his pointy knees into Nick's chest.

Those who follow Oklahoma City closely say Nick takes three times as many charging fouls as anyone on the Thunder roster. "It's a good play for our defense," he said. "It's better than a blocked shot, because you get the ball back, and you get a foul on someone on the other team. On a block, you might get the ball back, and you might not. And you don't draw a foul."

Nick is also one of the league's most underrated defenders—

a "glue-guy" who usually takes on the other team's best forward. His top-notch defensive skills are why he's paid in the $11 million a year range—which is close to All-Star numbers. A native Iowan who helped Kansas University reach two consecutive Final Fours (2002 and 2003), Nick's been called the ultimate hard-hat player.

Nick and his wife, Robbie, have hosted several charity events in Oklahoma City, most notably an annual Passion for Fashion benefit for AIDS foundations in the area. He became interested in helping fight AIDS after traveling to Johannesburg, South Africa, with Basketball Without Borders, which partnered with Habitat for Humanity and the Sky Foundation, which helps people with the HIV virus.

While in Johannesburg, Nick and Robbie, a microbiology major in college, witnessed firsthand how AIDS has ravaged families in South Africa and left so many children orphaned. The visit to South Africa inspired them to organize a fashion show benefit and silent auction, which has become a big hit in Oklahoma City since the first one in 2009.

But don't ask Nick to walk down the runway in a smart suit.

"Luckily, I've got the excuse that they've got no clothes that fit me," he said. "There's no big-and-tall line [in the fashion world]. There's nothing for me to model."

Actually, Nick is modeling Christ to those attending the annual charity event on behalf of orphaned children.

KEVIN DURANT
OKLAHOMA CITY THUNDER

While Nick Collison is the blue-collar, in-the-trenches player every team needs, Kevin Durant, Nick's teammate with the Oklahoma City Thunder, is the go-to-guy at crunch time, the big-time player who understands the responsibility of being "the guy" to carry the team. As one of the NBA's rising stars, he accepts the spotlight and the accolades, but as a young Christian man of faith, he doesn't seek the fame and attention.

It's hard to escape fame and attention, though, when you're a two-time NBA scoring leader. His game is smooth and seamless, a mixture of grace, class, and force. He's the face of the Oklahoma City Thunder franchise.

"In short, Kevin Durant is endorsement gold right now because he's good, he's new, he's young, he's intelligent, he's humble, and he's the centerpiece of a rags-to-riches story that has made him a hero to the citizens of Oklahoma City," wrote Patrick Rishe in *Forbes* magazine.

During the 2010–11 playoffs, Kevin showed up at post-game news conferences wearing a Nike backpack that will be part of his KD III line that's coming out during the 2011–12 season. Eventually, the inevitable question came from the back: "Hey, Kevin, what's in your backpack?"

Well, I've got my iPad, my earphones, my phone chargers—and my Bible.

Actually, the Bible was a recent addition to his backpack, but more on that later.

Kevin was raised in a Maryland suburb of Washington, DC. His mother and grandmother cared for him and his older brother Tony after their father left the family when Kevin was eight months old. As Kevin was growing up, he was always the tallest person in his class, but his grandmother Barbara consoled him, saying that his height would be a blessing— just wait and see.

He didn't have to wait long.

Kevin was a phenomenal basketball player from a young age, and when he was in middle school, he joined an AAU team. His AAU coach, Taras "Stink" Brown, laid down several rules, and Rule No. 1 was "no pickup games"—because his coach thought they engendered bad habits. Instead, Coach Brown gave Kevin a set of drills to perform. During his summer breaks, Kevin was often in the gym eight hours a day.

Kevin played his freshman and sophomore years at Montrose Christian High in Rockville, Maryland, where he was so good that his older teammates threatened to stop passing the ball to him because they didn't want Kevin to show them up. He later transferred to Oak Hill Academy in Mouth of Wilson, Virginia, where he played well enough to be named a McDonald's All-American. His shooting and driving skills were unmatched among prep players.

The University of Texas won the recruiting war for Kevin. As an eighteen-year-old freshman, Kevin controlled the flow of the game—and there was never a reason to call for a set play when he was on the floor. He posted twenty 30-point games, was named the Associated Press College Player of the Year, and won the Naismith and Wooden awards.

And promptly declared himself eligible for the 2007 NBA draft after one college season.

The Seattle SuperSonics (who would become the Oklahoma City Thunder) took Kevin with the second overall pick in the draft. He would become the NBA Rookie of the Year.

For a 6-foot, 9-inch player, Kevin has an usually long wingspan of 7 feet, 5 inches. Think about what impressive wingspan means to his game: with his arms outstretched on defense, he is eight inches *wider* than he is tall, which gives him the appearance of a windmill with four blades. As for the offensive side of the court, his long arms and quick first step make him a nearly unstoppable force. Whether he's pulling up for a jumper or slashing through the lane, he makes it look easy—as most scoring champions do.

Some people believe Kevin could break Kareem Abdul-Jabbar's all-time NBA scoring record of 38,387 points. Kevin has one advantage that could help him break Abdul-Jabbar's record. Kareem stayed at UCLA for four years, so the great center didn't turn pro until he was twenty-two years old. Kevin will be twenty-three years old at the start of his fifth NBA season, giving him a three-season leg up on Abdul-Jabbar.

Through his first four seasons, Kevin had a lifetime scoring average of 25.9 points per game, and he figures to up his point-per-game average in coming years. Since Abdul-Jabbar averaged 24.3 points per game over a twenty-year career, Kevin would have to . . . well, the mathematic permutations are numerous.

But back to how the black leather Bible with his name engraved on the front cover got into his Nike backpack.

Kevin's strong faith comes from how his mother and grandmother brought him up. He says he went to church a lot when he was young, but as year-round basketball took up so much time in his adolescence, he attended church less. When he arrived in the NBA, a Christian teammate named Kevin Ollie took him under his wing and helped him feel more comfortable about talking about his faith, about praying for others out loud, and about attending chapels before games. It has helped that there were a half-dozen players on the Thunder who took their faith seriously and were walking with the Lord.

Kevin comes across as a down-to-earth humble player, a guy you won't catch pounding his chest and getting in the grills of opponents. When he was asked how he appeared to stay humble while living and working in a world where it's easy to get caught up in the hype of fame and fortune that defines the NBA, Kevin said, "It's tough, man. I can't lie about that. But I always kind of pinch myself and say that any day this can be done. In the Bible, [it says] the Lord exalts humility, and that's one thing I try to be all the time. When I'm talking in front of people or when people tell me I'm great, I [remind myself that I] can always be better. I've just got to be thankful to the Lord for the gifts He's given me. My gift back to Him is to always be humble and to always try to work as hard as I can."

Kevin started toting his Bible around in March 2011 after making a commitment to read Scripture passages at his locker before games. He told reporters that he wants to grow spiritually with the Lord, especially after a Thunder team chaplain stressed the difference reading the Bible each day can make in one's life.

"I'm keeping strong at it, just trying to make my walk with faith a little better," he said. "That's making me a better person, opening my eyes to things. I'm also maturing as a person. I'm just trying to grow."

Growing spiritually, growing into one of the elite basketball players in the world, Kevin Durant is someone to keep your eyes on—and pray for.

GREIVIS VASQUEZ
MEMPHIS GRIZZLIES

When Greivis Vasquez attends the NBA chapels before every game, he enjoys praying with opposing players because he enjoys being with other believers so much.

"I've got Jesus in my heart," he told Bill Sorrell, a Memphis-based sportswriter. "I put everything in his hands. I live out of grace."

Greivis grew up playing street basketball in the barrios of Caracas, Venezuela. He and his family lived in a down-trodden neighborhood known as El Coche, where the young boys would huddle up and watch basketball on televisions so small that they could barely make out the players running up and down the court.

Greivis was such a flashy dribbler that his friends called him *Callejero*, or street-baller. Seeing how big and tall Greivis was growing during adolescence, Venezuelan sports ministers plucked him out of the barrios and put him into the national development program.

As Greivis' skills progressed, his family made the tough decision to send him to the United States so he could further his basketball skills. They enrolled him at Montrose Christian Academy in Rockville, Maryland—a private high school known for its basketball prowess. "Your potential is God's gift to you," begins the program's motto. "How you choose to use your potential is your gift to God."

When Greivis arrived in the United States, he didn't know how to speak English or anything about a personal relationship with Jesus Christ. He quickly picked up English, and he was introduced to a personal relationship with Christ, which left Greivis a changed young man.

Greivis went on to play college ball at the University of Maryland, where the 6-foot, 6-inch point guard became the first-ever Atlantic Coast Conference player to score at least 2,000 points (2,171), ring up 750 assists (772), and grab 600 rebounds (647). In 2010, he won the Bob Cousy Award as the nation's best point guard.

The Memphis Grizzlies drafted Greivis in the first round of the 2010 NBA draft, and his rookie year went well for him. He received more and more minutes as the season wore on, especially in the playoffs, where Memphis went much further than anyone expected before losing to Oklahoma City and Greivis' former teammate from Montrose Christian High, Kevin Durant.

Greivis is the third Venezuelan to play in the NBA, but his countrymen—Carl Herrera and Oscar Torres—were journeymen players who didn't see much action during their short two-year careers. After Greivis' better-than-average rookie season, he has a strong shot at becoming the first impact player from his country. He's known for his instinctive nature on the court and ability to make things happen.

Maybe God has bigger plans for Greivis. In the interviews he's given, he certainly hasn't shown any reluctance to talk about being a Christian. It must help that there are other Christians on the Grizzlies team—like Xavier Henry, Ishmael Smith, and Rudy Gay, who recites Philippians 4:13 before every free throw: "I can do all things through him who strengthens me." Greivis has memorized Scripture, too—the entire eighth chapter of Romans.

Asked how his Christian faith has helped him in the

NBA, Greivis replied, "It helps me in every aspect of my life. I have a sense of peace because I know God has blessed me so much. I thank Jesus every day, no matter what happens, good or bad. My faith is what got me to where I am today."

Greivis is active on Twitter, where he routinely talks about his faith in Spanish or English—sometime in both languages—like the time he tapped out the following message: EASY WITH THAT BRO. JESUS ES UN CABALLO!" (*Caballo* means rider or horseman, but in this context, the phrase is Venezuelan slang meaning "He's a big guy.")

Other tweets are more straightforward, like this one: "On my way to church. Thank you God for another day."

At last count, thirty-five thousand people were following Greivis on Twitter.

Maybe a few of them went to church that Sunday after reading his tweet.

JEFF RYAN
CHAPLAIN OF THE ORLANDO MAGIC

Jeff Ryan is part of an NBA program that places a chaplain with every team in the league. Many fans don't realize that a chapel service is held one hour before every NBA game—regular season and playoffs—and that players from *both* teams are welcome to attend.

This open invitation makes pro basketball different from other major sports, where players from opposing teams are kept separate during chapel services. NFL players have the option of attending a chapel service—just for their team—on the night before their games. Major League Baseball chapels are held in each team's locker rooms on Sunday mornings. Ditto for the NHL.

But in the NBA, one hour before tip-off, players from each team are invited to meet near the home and visitor locker rooms. It could be in an extra locker room or even the dressing room of the team mascot. Attendance is voluntary.

The home-team chaplain greets the players, and might lead an a cappella song. Then he speaks for ten to fifteen minutes, teaching from the Bible. Topics range from overcoming life's challenges to a reprise of the Gospel message, but the basic goal is to equip players to live lives that glorify God—especially by encouraging them to remain strong in the face of temptation.

At the end of the chapel, players might share a prayer request or ask a question about the message. Discussions must move quickly: whatever direction the chaplain takes, the mini-service must end promptly since players must be on court shortly to warm up for the game.

After they loosen up, players approach midcourt for the opening tip-off. And once the referee tosses the ball in the air, players from both teams—some of whom were seated in the same room discussing God's love less than an hour earlier—try to outrace, outhustle, and generally outshine their opponents—which is one of the beauties of competition.

Jeff said he's never had any issues with players from two teams meeting together before game time. They understand that professional rivalries don't matter in chapel, because that's a time allotted for God.

"As much as these guys are competitors, they realize that there are only four hundred professional basketball players in the NBA," Jeff said "Playing is a privilege, not a birthright. They worked hard to get into that room. They know they are paid to perform, and they are going to play hard."

NBA chaplains like Jeff are volunteers, not part of the front-office staff. They're usually pastors or involved in some form of full-time Christian ministry. One is even a former player: Andrew Lang, the Atlanta Hawks chaplain, who played twelve NBA seasons as a solid, consistent force in the low post. Whatever their background, chaplains present the Word of God to players with love and grace. They plant the seed, but God makes it grow. They see their ministry as sharing the Gospel, trying to encourage players and keep them strong.

"It's a great ministry, but it's also a humbling ministry," Jeff said. "I think the most important thing about being a chaplain is that it's about the message and not the messenger. As a chaplain, as a pastor, I'm irrelevant—but the message of God is relevant. That's what we're called to do—share the Good News. For some guys, we're just planting that one seed that will grow sometime down the road. For those guys who really embrace Christ, and live for Christ, our hope and prayer is that we will be good ministers for them."

MONTY WILLIAMS
HEAD COACH OF THE NEW ORLEANS HORNETS

At thirty-nine years of age, he was the youngest head coach in the NBA during the 2010–11 season, but for someone so young, Monty Williams is close friends with his mortality—and Jesus Christ.

Tavares Montgomery "Monty" Williams was a nineteen-year-old sophomore at Notre Dame and a starter on the Fighting Irish basketball team. At the start of preseason practice in 1990, he underwent a routine physical. The doctor frowned when he listened to Monty's heartbeat. Something didn't sound right.

The doctor sent Monty to a cardiologist, who determined that he suffered from hypertrophic cardiomyopathy (HCM), a structural defect resulting in the heart muscle being bigger than it's supposed to be. Intense physical activity—like running up and down a basketball court—can trigger a heart attack, perhaps a fatal one, in people with HCM.

In the fall of 1990, the basketball world was still in shock after watching Hank Gathers, an All-American forward for Loyola Marymount University, collapse on the basketball court on March 4 of that year.

During the first half of a West Coast Conference tournament game against the University of Portland, Gathers ran the court in LMU's fast-break attack, taking a long lob pass in midair and slamming the basketball through the hoop. The home crowd cheered the athletic play, and Gathers dropped back on defense. Suddenly, he collapsed at midcourt with a thud. The crowd gasped.

Gathers' body started going into convulsions, and when

the team doctor and coaches rushed onto the court, it was apparent that something was terribly wrong. The sight of Gathers' bewildered look about what was happening to him—all captured by cameras that night—was a sad spectacle.

Gathers was later declared dead on arrival at a Los Angeles hospital. The autopsy revealed that he had suffered from hypertrophic cardiomyopathy.

Notre Dame officials weren't going to take any chances with their star 6-foot, 8-inch forward from Forest Heights, Maryland. "Heart Condition Ends Notre Dame Player's Career," read the headline in the *Los Angeles Times* on September 29, 1990. Monty was quoted in the story as saying he was grateful his condition was diagnosed, even though that meant he would never play basketball again.

"I'm lucky to get a second chance," he said, "I wasn't on the court and died like Hank Gathers did."

But that gratefulness turned to bitterness and frustration as the reality of losing his basketball career overwhelmed him. Monty's mother had raised him in a Christian home, and he was a believer at the time of his diagnosis—but he was still crushed.

Friends quickly jumped off the Monty Williams bandwagon in South Bend, Indiana. Nobody wanted to hang out with a has-been—except for his girlfriend, Ingrid Lacy, the daughter of a preacher.

During that dark time, Monty rededicated his life to Christ. He and Ingrid spent hours walking around the Notre Dame campus in introspective prayer—begging the Lord for a miracle.

Meanwhile, Monty continued to play in pickup games at the Knute Rockne Memorial Gym on campus, telling friends that if he were to die, then at least it would be on a basketball court. He'd just wake up in heaven, that's all.

Two years passed, and Monty couldn't feel any ill effects from his heart condition. Then he heard that the National Institutes of Health (NIH) in Bethesda, Maryland, was studying the risk posed to athletes with HCM. He contacted NIH and asked if he could participate in the study, which meant enduring three days of exhaustive medical and stress tests. The results stunned the doctors. They couldn't find anything wrong with his heart.

When Monty heard the news, he dropped to his knees, praying and crying. "To this day, the doctors can't understand what happened," he said. "But God healed my heart. Medicine has its place in the world. Faith has its place, too. And faith overrides medicine."

In 1993, Monty resumed his basketball career at Notre Dame and averaged 22.4 points per game as the only star on a lousy Fighting Irish team. He could have played another year of college ball but elected to turn pro. Several teams passed him over because of his medical history, but the New York Knicks selected him with the twenty-fourth pick of the 1994 NBA draft.

The Knicks organization, no doubt spooked by the death of Boston Celtics player Reggie Lewis a year earlier, after he collapsed and died of HCM while playing basketball, told Monty he would have to pass another round of cardiological tests before they'd sign him.

Monty passed his physical with flying colors and went on to play nine years in the NBA for five different teams before a knee injury sent him to the bench permanently. One of his coaches, Gregg Popovich of the San Antonio Spurs, always thought of Monty as one of those coachable players who understood the game and had the correct don't-get-too-high-or-get-too-low demeanor. Coach Popovich hired Monty as a bench coach, and he made a smooth transition into coaching and mentoring players.

Monty later moved on to Portland, where he worked as an assistant coach for the Trail Blazers, and in the summer of 2010, he was named the head coach for the floundering New Orleans Hornets. New Orleans promptly made a big turn-around during the 2010–11 season. The Hornets finished the regular season with a 46–36 record and returned to the playoffs, where they put a scare into the defending champion Los Angeles Lakers before bowing out in six games.

With the visibility of being an NBA head coach, Monty welcomed questions about what was really important in his life, which gave him a platform to talk about his faith and act it out on the court. For instance, he doesn't use bad language when yelling at referees—or when trying to get a player's attention. He told interviewers he reads his Bible every day and that the Word was as much a part of his existence as his wife, Ingrid—whom he married in 1995—and their five children.

He and Ingrid, along with youth pastor Dave Bullis and his wife, Kaci, wrote a devotional called *Look Again 52: One Scripture, Every Day, Each Week, for One Year*, which was released in the fall of 2010.

"We came up with a tool that will help people take certain verses and chew on them for a week," Monty said. "The book came out of a problem. I struggled, and we felt like the Lord gave us this idea to come up with a tool. It cost me a bunch of money to do the book because we self-published it, but being in the NBA, I'd blow that much money on a car and a dog, so it wasn't a big deal to do it."

Monty has run into people who have read *Look Again 52* and told him the book ministered to them. "It puts it in perspective that God could use a jerk like me, with all my shortcomings and blemishes, to do something that helps somebody that I would never meet," Monty said.

PAT WILLIAMS
GENERAL MANAGER OF THE ORLANDO MAGIC

Not only are there players playing with purpose in the NBA, as well as coaches coaching with purpose (like Monty Williams, Avery Johnson of the New Jersey Nets, and Paul Westphal of the Sacramento Kings), but there are also front office personnel of faith working behind the scenes to put the best possible team on the floor.

One of those Christian executives is Pat Williams, the senior vice president of the Orlando Magic. Nobody wrings more out of a day than Pat—and that is no hyperbole. Consider what this seventy-one-year-old Renaissance man has accomplished since he came into the NBA in 1968. He's:

- been the general manager of four NBA teams: the Chicago Bulls, Atlanta Hawks, Philadelphia 76ers, and the Orlando Magic, which he co-founded in 1987.
- brought professional basketball to Orlando—a medium-sized city filled with amusement parks and a transient population. He was ridiculed for trying to sell basketball in a football fanatical state, but it was Pat who had the last laugh.
- written seventy-five books in the past four decades, mainly on the topics of leadership, teamwork, good business practices, being a better parent, and living a successful and rewarding life.
- carved out a successful career as one of America's top motivational and inspirational speakers, speaking 150 times a year to Fortune 500 companies like Allstate, American Express, Disney,

Nike, and Tyson Foods, as well as to nonprofit organizations.

- raised nineteen children—and that is not a typographical error. He and his first wife, Jill, had four children on their own and adopted fourteen—from four foreign countries—during the 1970s and 1980s. His second wife, Ruth, brought one child into their marriage. At one point, sixteen of his kids were teenagers living under his roof at the same time, and Pat was single-parenting them. "That's when I understood why some animals eat their young," he quipped.

- run in fifty-eight marathons, including the Boston Marathon and the New York Marathon. At the time of this writing, his most recent was the Walt Disney Marathon in Orlando in early 2011—his third in four months.

Two days before the Disney Marathon, Pat visited his doctor for his annual physical. Blood was drawn and tests were done. Then he jogged 26.2 miles on a course that ran through all four theme parks inside the Magic Kingdom. But when he woke up a few days later, he felt a lot more than the usual soreness. His back was on fire.

During a return visit to see his doctor, Pat was told that abnormalities had shown up in his blood work. Further results revealed that he had multiple myeloma, a cancer of the plasma cells in his bone marrow. One of the symptoms of multiple myeloma is extreme back pain.

Pat was referred to Dr. Robert Reynolds, a leading oncologist in Orlando, who told him he was confident that Pat's multiple myeloma—also known as MM—had been detected in its early stages and could be treated. Dr. Reynolds told him that while multiple myeloma could be treated but not cured, he had a 70 to 75 percent chance of remission.

With that information as a background, Pat asked if he could tell his own story, and that seemed like an easy request to agree to:

PAT WILLIAMS IN HIS OWN WORDS

It's funny that this is a basketball book, yet my opening topic is baseball. But baseball was my prime sport when I was growing up in a sports-minded home in Wilmington, Delaware. Baseball, to paraphrase Sammy Sosa, was very, very good to me. Baseball got me through Wake Forest University, where I played catcher. Upon my graduation, I signed a contract with the Philadelphia Phillies and spent two years catching in their farm system, during the 1962 and 1963 seasons.

When I saw the handwriting on the wall—that I wasn't destined for the Major Leagues—I sought out other opportunities in the Phillies minor league system. I spent four years as the general manager of their farm club in Spartanburg, South Carolina. We had enormous success in Spartanburg during the mid-1960s, setting attendance records and winning national honors in minor league baseball.

I loved coming up with promotions that would pack Duncan Park with lots of baseball fans. One season, the Phillies sent us two pitchers out of spring training—guys named John Parker and John Penn. Well, back then Parker Pens were a big deal, so I conjured up Parker-Penn night where everyone in attendance would get a free pen.

Anything to have a little fun at the ballpark in those care-free days.

I was in my mid-twenties and searching and seeking to get to the top of my profession, yet with all the success I was enjoying, there was this certain emptiness as well. I surely relished all the honors and all the success, but there was soul-searching and questioning on my part.

There has got to be more than what I am experiencing here, I thought to myself. As I was pondering those larger-than-life thoughts, different people came into my life—like the "King of Squat," Olympic weightlifting champion Paul Anderson, and former Major League Baseball players Bobby Malkmus and Bobby Richardson, the great Yankee second baseman. They all talked to me about Christianity and hearing what they said appealed to me.

Just prior to my twenty-eighth birthday, I made a deci-sion: *I want to get into this Christian thing.* I accepted Christ into my life. It was a radical transformation for me and changed my life totally and immediately. Anybody who says there can't be instant conversion, well, I tell them that's not true. One day I was walking one path, and fifteen minutes later I was heading in a whole different direction.

I obviously had a huge transformation in my life. I had been pushing and maneuvering, but trying to get to the top on my own wasn't working out the way I thought it would. When I accepted Christ, I said, "Lord, You do what You want with my life. I'm just going to surrender it. I am going to take my hands off the wheel, and You take over from here."

With that mind-set, I walked into the ballpark one day in July 1968 and found out there was a message for me to return a phone call to a man named Jack Ramsay. I recognized the name. He had been the longtime basketball coach at St. Joseph's in Philadelphia before becoming the general manager of the 76ers.

What could Jack Ramsay want? I wondered. I knew *of* him, but I certainly didn't *know* him. When I returned the phone call, Jack explained to me that he was taking over the coaching duties for the 76ers in the fall of 1968, in addition to his GM job. He needed somebody to run his front office while he concentrated on coaching the team. Would I be interested?

I gulped and thought, *Me*? I was twenty-eight years old, running a minor-league baseball team in South Carolina. What did I know about NBA basketball? But Jack had checked me out, and after bringing me to Philadelphia for two interviews, offered me the job as business manager, which was basically running the front office.

It was a huge jump from minor-league baseball to running an NBA basketball operation day to day. But I learned a great deal and had a wonderful experience. Twelve months later, another door opened. This time, the owners of the Chicago Bulls contacted me and said they needed a general manager to run their team. Was I interested?

Jack Ramsay let me out of my contract with Philadelphia, and in the late summer of 1969, I moved to Chicago and took over the GM duties for the Bulls. I later moved on to the Atlanta Hawks and the Philadelphia 76ers again before finally landing in Orlando, where I helped launch an NBA expansion franchise in 1986 and bring professional basketball to central Florida.

Along the way, I have been responsible for the day-to-day general manager duties, which have entailed everything from contract negotiations to the draft, team trades, halftime shows, promotions, and even the exhibition schedule.

During my forty-three-year soirée through the National Basketball Association, I have witnessed the sport grow and become a worldwide entity. I have seen the influx of foreign-born players into the NBA. I have seen the league office in New York City grow from four full-time employees to about twenty-five hundred employees worldwide. Basketball has become a huge global sporting endeavor, and being part of that for four-and-a-half decades has been staggering but rewarding in many ways.

Throughout these years I have been very fortunate to develop a side career. When I initially arrived in Orlando twenty-five years ago to help start the Magic expansion franchise, Orlando was just beginning to grow as a convention city and as a destination resort. Speaking opportunities seemed to pop up for me from the corporate world. I started speaking on leadership, teamwork, quality of life, living to your full potential, and what it takes to be a winner.

I speak probably one hundred fifty times a year to different groups in Orlando and around the country—and in some cases other countries. The Magic ownership, starting with Rich DeVos and his family, have been supportive and given me the freedom to do that.

Probably the highlight has been speaking at two Billy Graham Crusades—one in Chicago and one in Syracuse, New York, back in the 1970s and 1980s. I'll never forget seeing Dr. Graham in his heyday, as well as Cliff Barrows and

George Beverly Shea. Feeling the Lord's presence as I walked into each evening session—with the four-thousand-voice choirs and forty thousand people sitting there—oh boy, I'm not sure that I'll ever experience anything like that again this side of heaven.

As my speaking career grew, it led to opportunities to write books. My seventieth book was released in early 2011, and I have more books I want to write. My speaking and writing careers have allowed me to meet fascinating people in corporate America and provided me enough money to get my children through college—not an easy task when there were nineteen of them. Now that all my children are adults and marrying and forming families of their own, my focus is on getting my grandchildren through high school and college, which I have committed to do for them.

Yes, the ending of my first marriage in the mid-1990s was very difficult for me and very difficult for our eighteen children. My ex-wife just didn't want to continue the marriage, and there was nothing I could do about it. We had written about marriage and had been very visible in the Christian community, so it was an embarrassing and difficult time in my life when we separated and divorced.

I ended up single parenting eighteen children for a few years, but I was sinking fast. Then Ruth, who would become my second wife, came along and basically saved my bacon. I refer to her now as "St. Ruth," and she remains St. Ruth today—with nineteen adult children and eight grandchildren, dealing with daily issues I could never deal with on my own. She has been a lifesaver for all us.

Those years in the mid-1990s were times of adversity for

me and my family, which has given me a forum to talk about how we can deal with adversity and use it to develop strength. When winners experience setbacks, disappointments, or failures, they don't waste those difficult times. Instead, they learn and grow and take advantage of those experiences to become smarter, wiser, and more capable of going through the tough times the next time around.

Even though I had been speaking on adversity for many years, little did I realize that I would be given an opportunity to live out my own words in front of the world beginning in 2011.

It all started when I visited my doctor for my yearly physical two days before the Disney Marathon. When my blood work results came back, my doctor said, "There is something that needs further checking. I would encourage you to get on it right away."

Over the next few weeks, I saw a series of specialists, including Dr. Robert Reynolds, an oncologist here in the Orlando area. After reviewing my results, he sat me down and explained that I had an illness called multiple myeloma.

"I have never heard of that," I said. "What is it?"

Dr. Reynolds explained that multiple myeloma is a cancerous condition of the bone marrow and not a common illness (which was interesting to hear now that I've heard from every MM patient in America!).

Dr. Reynolds started me on chemotherapy treatment immediately, and then I had to make a huge decision. What do I do about informing my children? The Magic organization? And the public? I knew that sooner or later the story would start leaking and hit the newspapers. In February 2011, I decided to get it all out in front of people.

The Magic organization called a press conference for me, and I stood at the podium, with Dr. Reynolds by my side, and announced that I was dealing with multiple myeloma. I remember saying that I have been talking for years to audiences about dealing with adversity and tough times, but now I would get a chance to live it out. I also talked a great deal about my faith and the importance of living for the Lord. I said that when I received the news of my cancer diagnosis, I could have shook my fist in the Lord's face and turned angrily away from Him. You know—*Why me? How could you do this to me?* Instead, I decided to make a flying leap into His lap and hug Him around the neck and never let go.

In many ways, I'm grateful for this news about my cancer diagnosis and its timing. We caught it early. It's certainly nothing I would have planned or wanted, but learning I have cancer has certainly drawn me closer to the Lord and given me a closer walk with Him.

In addition, I feel I have been called to a ministry of encouraging and uplifting other people. Every day I get a phone call or an e-mail from someone dealing with cancer or other health-related issues. I try to respond to all of them with an optimistic, upbeat attitude, to pray with them, and to help give them a spark to keep fighting hard to regain their health. I am also convinced that every family in America has been touched in some form or fashion with cancer. I feel the Lord wants me to be a cheerleader for as many cancer patients as I can.

I made good progress throughout 2011 after submitting to several months of chemo treatments. One of the nurses at the clinic really encouraged me, saying, "Listen, these chemo treatments take about an hour each time, twice a week, and that's it. The rest of the week is yours. So don't sit on the sidelines. You may not feel 100 percent, but go out there at 80 percent and go on with your life."

I have been feeling more energetic with each week as I seek to live a normal life. I resumed traveling and flying here and there to do my talks, and I have several books on the docket to write. I may not feel perfect, but I'm going out and playing at the level God has given me. Obviously, I am grateful for the enormous amount of prayer support around the country, from friends and strangers alike who have reached out to encourage me.

Once I began chemotherapy, I started keeping a journal. Who knows? I've heard that people are already anticipating a book about this whole experience, so I'll keep good notes and see where this leads.

When I'm out speaking and young people hear my story, they often ask me, *What is the key to having a good life?* I tell them to figure out what they love to do more than anything in the world and then come up with a way to get paid every two weeks for doing it. When you max out every day of your life, you'll have life by the throat.

Another question I'm often asked is, "What makes a good GM?"

Well, you're never off duty. You are working 24/7. Your stomach is churning every day when things are going well *and* when they are not going well. It's fortunate that I became a Christian before I became a general manager; otherwise I could not have functioned in this world. The pressures are too intense, the tension is too nerve-racking.

But the Lord has given me a certain peace and a certain calmness through it all. It helps that I view my work as a ministry. Sure, winning is important. I would not still be in this business after forty-three years if the teams I worked for hadn't won a whole lot more games than they lost. But I always viewed my position as an opportunity to impact people through the power of sports. Having that thought in the back of my mind gives me a different perspective. I want to win as badly as anybody, and I'm willing to work hard, but I've always felt this has been the Lord's work.

Part of that work involves evaluating talent—who you bring to play on your team. You have to draft well. You have to trade well. You have to make good decisions in free agency. You have to have good people around you, and you have to listen to them, trust them, and give them the freedom to be good decision-makers on your behalf.

You must have talent, but character counts enormously. When you get caught up with talented players who are deficient in the character department, you end up spending all your time putting out fires that are due to character issues. That takes time, and inevitably you end up neglecting your good-character guys, which diverts from everything you're trying to do.

At the Orlando Magic, we do everything in our power to draft talent *with* character, and when you get those two in combination, you know you are going to have wonderful success. It's not easy to discover a player's character, however, which is why we must do an enormous amount of research. We have a whole lot more scouts than we used to. We had one scout when I started out with Chicago, Atlanta, and Philly. We probably have eight or ten scouts on the Magic payroll now.

We go back and try to check into each player's youth and spend as much time as we can around his college campus. We talk to the people who have coached that player when he was a young person. It helps if we can do psychological testing, too. It's not a perfect formula, but we spend as much time as we can evaluating and digging deep into a youngster's past.

With the Internet, that's much easier these days. It seems like we can find out everything about everybody in the world. If a player spilled a cup of coffee in a Starbucks a few months ago, we probably have a report on that. When something more serious has happened in a player's past—such as a DUI or an assault arrest—we have to make a decision: was it youthful peccadilloes, was it a maturity issue, or was this part of a pattern?

The danger for scouts and general managers is that we are tempted by talent. I've sat in meetings where people say, *Well, I can overcome the character stuff.* At the end of the day, though, a kid's character is pretty well formed by the time he is a teenager. You have to be very careful, especially now that the game has become a worldwide sport. We have players coming from all over the world. How can we determine a player's character when he's grown up in France, Germany, or Turkey? That's why we have to be scouting on every continent, but it also comes down to asking the Lord for guidance.

I don't know where my life would be without that resource from above. I am convinced that everything that has happened on and off the basketball court started with the decision I made in February 1968 to turn my life over to Christ and let Him run with it and control it, which He has been doing very, very well for these many years.

I'm deeply thankful I was drafted onto His team.

OVERTIME

PISTOL PETE MARAVICH, THE PRODIGAL WHO PLAYED WITH PURPOSE

I (Mike Yorkey) loved playing basketball growing up in La Jolla, California, a seaside community about twenty minutes north of downtown San Diego.

In the Mediterranean climate and bucolic setting of La Jolla, the neighborhood gang and I could play outdoors year-round, although basketball was generally a Thanksgiving-to-Lent sport sandwiched between baseball and beach time. When I was in the fifth grade, my father constructed a free-standing wooden basketball standard that was low enough for us to dunk on. Playing on low rims didn't help my jump shot, but it was sure fun to stuff like Wilt "The Stilt" Chamberlain.

The low rim was strictly for horsing around. I made sure I played plenty of hoops on ten-foot rims because that was *real* basketball. I haven't forgotten how much joy I received from seeing my jump shots spring from my fingertips, suspend in midair for the longest time, and swish through the basket.

In the late 1960s, as I entered my teen years, the NBA awarded an expansion franchise to San Diego. The team was named the Rockets because Atlas rockets were made in San Diego, and since these massive liquid-fuel space launch vehicles blasted American astronauts into space, there was a lot of local pride. (If you're a younger reader, rockets were a big deal in the 1960s because of the "Space Race" to get a man on the moon before the Russians.) The Rockets would play only four seasons in San Diego, from 1967 to 1971, before moving to Houston.

The Rockets were horrible during their inaugural year, finishing with a 15–67 record, which, at that time, was the worst in NBA history. The team was populated with castoffs and journeymen like Art "Hambone" Williams and bald-as-a-billiard-ball Toby Kimball—although an interesting rookie guard with shaggy hair, big sideburns, and a Fu Manchu moustache, Pat Riley, was making some noise.

But not enough noise to win many games. With such a lousy team, professional basketball was greeted with yawns in laid-back San Diego, a place of surf, sun, and sand. Most people decided they had better things to do than go see a professional basketball game.

One Saturday night during the Rockets' first season in San Diego, my father and I decided at the last minute to go check out the team. The Cincinnati Royals, led by the Big O (Oscar Robertson) were in town. I was in junior high at the time.

My father and I walked right up to the ticket window to buy tickets—there was no line—and asked what was available.

"We have two seats on the floor," said the ticket seller.

"How much?" my father asked.

"Five bucks each."

Considering that actor Jack Nicholson pays $5,500 for a pair of courtside tickets at a Lakers game these days, ten bucks was a bargain, even in 1967 terms.

We took them. That was the first time—and the last— that I ever sat courtside for an NBA game. Listening to the Big O direct traffic and tell his guys where to go was a real treat. (With just a few thousand fans inside the San Diego Sports Arena, crowd noise was minimal.) He moved players around like they were pawns on a chessboard. I loved the way these amazing athletes flicked snap passes, played above the rim, and routinely made difficult shots look easy. That evening cemented my love for NBA basketball.

Meanwhile, I kept honing my game to where I was good enough to play on the La Jolla High varsity team. But I was one of those under-sized and under-talented players who wasn't going anywhere. I knew I had no future in basketball—tennis would become my sport anyway—but that didn't diminish my ardor for the game.

I pretty much quit playing basketball after high school— until I started working for Focus on the Family in 1986. I was hired as the editor of *Focus on the Family* magazine, which had a monthly circulation of well over a million readers.

Focus on the Family is a non-profit Christian organization founded in 1977 by Dr. James Dobson, the author of bestselling books such as *Dare to Discipline* and *The Strong-Willed Child*. The main focus of the ministry was Dr. Dobson's daily radio show, which featured him and a guest talking about parenting and family issues. The ministry, which employed around 350 people at the time, was based in Dr. Dobson's hometown of Arcadia, California, an upscale community thirteen miles northeast of downtown Los Angeles and sitting on the border of Pasadena.

I soon learned that Dr. Dobson, fifty years old at the time, was also a basketball nut. He was crazy about the game, so much so that the job description for Gary Lydic, Focus' human resources director at the time, included the heavy responsibility of making sure enough players showed up before work to play five-on-five half-court games three mornings a week. The venue was a nice, well-appointed gymnasium on the grounds of First Church of the Nazarene of Pasadena, where Dr. Dobson's first cousin, H. B. London, served as pastor.

"Let me tell you, it was an incredible responsibility to have players organized for those games three times a week," Gary said. "When I had my list made up, I'd call everyone the day before and say, 'Guys, you know how important this is to the Doctor to be there tomorrow morning. There is no way you cannot be there, unless you're playing on one leg.' It wasn't so easy to get to everyone in those days before cell phones, but if somebody didn't show up, it was my fault. I hated to get those early morning phone calls from Dr. Dobson saying that not enough players had showed up to play."

Shortly after Focus hired me, I was put on Gary's call list. (I think I mentioned to Dr. Dobson that I had played some high school basketball and would love the opportunity to scrape off the rust and play again.) I learned quickly that when Dr. Dobson invited you play basketball, you had better be ready to play at 6:30 a.m. at "First Naz Paz."

What followed was an hour and fifteen minutes of

quick-burst five-on-five half-court games. There were usually enough players to field four teams, so we had two half
courts going. First team to score ten baskets won the game.
Winners would play winners and losers would play losers.

I actually preferred half-court basketball, as did Dr. Dobson. I felt that keeping both teams on the same side of the
court—but having to take the ball back beyond the top of the
key following each change of possession—made for a better
game. Often when amateurs and weekend warriors play full-
court basketball, the game degenerates into a series of two-
on-one fast breaks, which are no fun.

With half-court basketball, though, it was always five-on-
five with screens and movement and open jump shots—and
no "cherry pickers" taking off for the other rim and an un-
molested lay-up. I'm sure I worked up *more* of a sweat playing half-court hoops, and the competitive games certainly
satisfied my craving to play basketball. I also liked the "winners out" rule, where your team kept the ball after scoring.
That way, any team could make a late charge.

Dr. Dobson was a good player, especially for someone his
age. Give him an uncontested jump shot near the free throw
line, and he was money. Even though most guys in his pickup
games were fifteen or twenty years younger than Dr. Dobson,
he more than held his own. He used his height and size to his
physical advantage to jostle for rebounds and score easy baskets.

Another thing I remember about those early morning
games was that Dr. Dobson was very big on players calling
fouls on themselves. There was kind of an "honor system" we
all had to adhere to, meaning that if one of us made contact
with an opponent who was taking a shot, then we'd better

raise our hands and acknowledge the foul.

Dr. Dobson is 6 feet, 3 inches, so he was more of a forward while I, at my 5-foot, 9-inch height, was more of a guard. Sometimes, though, he'd break free and it would be up to me to contest his shot. If I hacked him or even gave him a little bump, I'd immediately raise my hand if and when the shot clanged off the rim so his team could retain possession. Hey, I called fouls on myself because I wanted to stay on the invite list!

There was one time, though, when I wasn't invited to play early morning basketball with Dr. Dobson and the rest of the guys. The date was January 5, 1988, the day when Pete Maravich was in town to tape a "Focus on the Family" radio program with Dr. Dobson. Pistol Pete had agreed to play a little pickup ball with Dr. Dobson and the guys at First Church of the Nazarene before going to the studio.

I was perfectly fine with not being invited to play that day—I knew my place. But if I had shown up at Parker Gym, I would have witnessed something I never would have forgotten—the sight of Pete Maravich, one of the most talented players ever to play the game, dying in Dr. Dobson's arms.

HEIR TO A DREAM

Pete Maravich wasn't the first player to dribble behind his back or make deft passes between his legs. But when the ball was in his hands, Pete was a mesmerizing showman.

Pistol Pete played basketball like no one before him, although some believe he paid a terrible price for putting his playground moves, circus shots, and hotdog passes on display. Many basketball purists felt he was more style than substance. In Pete's mind, though, if he could get you the ball with a chest pass or a behind-the-back bounce pass, why did it matter how he delivered the ball?

"If I have a chance to do the show or throw a straight pass, and we're going to get the basket either way," he once said, "I'm going to do the show."

Paul Westphal, who played in the NBA with Maravich before embarking on a long coaching career, compared Pete to an artist: "His canvas was the basketball floor, and his brush was his basketball."

Pete cultivated a freewheeling image that matched the tenor of the turbulent late '60s and early '70s. Even his dribbling wizardry—the double clutch and flip flap jack—was considered outrageous for his era. Yet with his Beatlesesque mop top of brown hair, trademark floppy socks, and a dead-eye shot that earned him the nickname "Pistol," he would become one of basketball's enigmatic icons. He *averaged* 44 points a game throughout his storied three-year career at Louisiana State University, but that could have easily been 50-plus points a game if there had been a three-point shot in college basketball when he played.

Peter Press Maravich was born June 22, 1947, the son of Serbian immigrants living in the steel town of Aliquippa, Pennsylvania. His father, Press, had grown up dirt poor at a time when he was expected to eke out a living in one of the huge gray steel mills that belched thick black smoke and polluted the upper Ohio River Valley.

Press viewed sports as his ticket out of the steel mills, and he threw himself into a game that was gaining popularity in the 1940s—basketball. After flying dozens of dangerous missions in the South Pacific as a U.S. naval pilot during World War II, he came home and played professional basketball with the Youngstown Bears of the National Basketball League (1945–46) and the Pittsburgh Ironmen of the Basketball Association of America (1946–47). These were the pre-NBA days, when salaries were miniscule.

Following marriage and the birth of Pete, Press needed something more secure than playing pro basketball to earn a few bucks. He turned to coaching and quickly reached the college ranks, but bubbling underneath the surface was a dream of what basketball and basketball players could become one day. His son, Pete Maravich, would become the embodiment of that dream, the realization of that vision. That's why Pete titled his 1987 autobiography *Heir to a Dream*.

Pete was a normal kid growing up, and he usually had some sort of ball in his hands. One day when Pete was seven years old, Press was shooting baskets in his yard in Clemson, South Carolina, where he worked as the head basketball coach at Clemson University. Pete came out and took a shot. He missed.

He was hooked. "Daddy, let me try again," he pleaded.

His father looked at him. "Pete, if you will let me teach you basketball, maybe one day you will play on the professional level like I did. Maybe you will be on a team that wins the world championship, and they will give you a big ring."

Pete's eyes lit up. He wanted that ring more than anything. He wanted to play basketball and earn fame and fortune.

Press had a willing subject to teach the fundamentals of basketball to. They went to work. Pete must have repeated his father's shooting mantra thousands of times: "fingertip control, backspin, and follow-through." The Clemson field house became the laboratory where Pete mastered the creative ball-handling drills his father had devised. Most were dribbling exercises with names like "scrambled egg" and "space clap." On weekends, young Pete dribbled and shot baskets eight to ten hours a day . . . until his fingertips were raw. He played games of three-on-three until he nearly dropped from hunger pangs.

The leather basketball almost became a natural extension of Pete's body. Everywhere Pete went, he took his basketball with him, bouncing it like a yo-yo.

"Whenever I went to the movies, I'd take my ball with me and be sure to get an end seat so I could dribble in the aisle while the movies were on," Pete wrote in a first-person article that appeared in *Sports Illustrated* in 1969, during his final season at LSU. "There were only a few people in the theater then. Clemson, South Carolina, wasn't the biggest metropolis in the world, you know. Those people in the theater were old and tired, and they looked like they'd been sitting there for three years. They didn't mind my dribbling—the floor was carpeted and I had a rubber ball—and I never got thrown out for it or anything.

"Later, about the fourth or fifth grade, I was still timid and shy around people—like a lot of kids my age—and I would practice in the gym all by myself. When you're in the gym alone, you know, you can do anything you want because nobody is there to stop you. I began finagling with the ball in there, fooling around with it and doing funny things. I would get bored with just shooting straight to the basket or dribbling around in circles.

"So I practiced different stuff with ball handling and dribbling, stuff that was exciting to me and much more fun. I would throw it off the wall and try to make a basket. I'd bounce it off the floor and up to the rim. I'd throw it over the rafters and try to bank it, stuff like that. Then I'd try passing against the wall, first throwing the ball behind my back, then through my legs and around my neck, aiming for a spot on the wall. Usually I made all kinds of difficult shots that seemed impossible to the rest of the kids when I would tell them about them."

Pete took his basketball to bed with him and practiced his shooting form before fatigue lulled him to sleep. After he got a bike for Christmas one year, he began learning to dribble while pedaling.

One time, his father took him for a car ride and drove at varying speeds while Pete leaned out the passenger window, trying to dribble the ball from the moving car. He also dribbled along sidewalks blindfolded and dribbled on railroad tracks, keeping the bouncing ball in the center of the three-inch-wide strips of iron rail. (Not easy to do, as Luke Ridnour would one day discover.)

Pete became so good at spinning the ball on his fingers that he once took a five-dollar bet that he could spin the ball on his fingers for one hour without stopping. After ten minutes of spinning the basketball on his index finger, the digit turned raw and started to bleed. He moved the spinning ball to the other fingers on his right hand—then his left. When all his fingertips became too tender to continue much further, he switched to his knuckles and thumbs to keep the spinning ball aloft—and collected his five bucks.

For much of his childhood and adolescence, Pete was devoted to dribbling, practicing his passes, and honing his jump shot along with the one-hand push, the set shot, and the hook. He became a student of the game, sitting beside his father in dozens of different college field houses, watching him chew on a white towel and periodically blow up at the referees.

Pete's stunning basketball skills earned him a spot on the high school team when he was in the eighth grade, a development his older teammates didn't take well. Remember, this was the early 1960s, and his style of "show time" basketball had never been seen before. Pete became the target of ridicule and was socially ostracized by his teammates, which was very difficult for him to take.

It wasn't until Pete's junior and senior years in high school that he gained acceptance from his teammates. As he poured in jump shots from every spot on the court, "Pistol Pete," as the local sportswriters tabbed him, became a blue-chip college basketball recruit. He was in the midst of a growth spurt that would take him to 6 feet, 5 inches tall—the perfect height for a playmaking, shooting guard.

Lots of schools wanted him, but there was a complication: during Pete's senior year of high school, his father had finagled a job offer to coach at Louisiana State University—a football school if there ever was one. There was an implicit *quid pro quo* between Press and LSU: *If you want this job, you better bring Pete with you.*

Pete wasn't thrilled to learn that. He didn't want to play for some doggone football school where the field house smelled like a barn. He wanted to play for the University of

West Virginia, where Jerry West—"Mr. Clutch" for the Los Angeles Lakers—had sharpened his game.

Press delivered an ultimatum to his son: *If you don't come play for me at LSU, don't ever come home again.*

Pete caved, and that's how he landed at Louisiana State. Despite taking his game to bayou country, he captured the nation's attention, very much like John, Paul, George, and Ringo had when they stepped off a plane at John F. Kennedy Airport in 1964. He was a great scorer who entertained crowds with between-the-legs passes and flashy dribbles that left bug-eyed defenders playing like someone had bound their ankles with rope. The 3,667 points he scored during his collegiate career is still a Division I record—and that despite the fact that he played only three years at LSU due to an NCAA rule at the time that prevented college freshmen from playing varsity basketball. That rule was changed in 1972.

When Pete's amazing college career was over, he signed what was then the largest pro contract in history with the Atlanta Hawks—$1.9 million. Pete sat at a press conference with famed sportscaster Howard Cosell and forty-two microphones and announced to the world, "I've arrived. Now all I need is that ring. Then I'll be happy for the rest of my days on earth."

THINGS DIDN'T WORK OUT AS EXPECTED

Pete Maravich never got his NBA championship ring.

For all his personal achievements and all the flair he put on display during his ten-year NBA career, Pete was never a big winner in the pros. Sure, he led the league in scoring one season, played in five NBA All-Star games, and averaged

24 points a game over his career, but Pistol Pete could never escape the perception that he played mostly for himself, that the team was secondary.

A former teammate, "Sweet Lou" Hudson, summed it up this way: "This man has been quicker than Jerry West or Oscar Robertson. He gets the ball up the floor better. He shoots as well. Raw talent–wise, he's the greatest who ever played. The difference comes down to style. He will be a loser, always, no matter what he does. That's his legacy. It never looked easy being Pete Maravich."

With his game underappreciated, his teams losing more than they were winning, Pete was miserable. Basketball had always been his god, his religion—the most important thing in his life. But he wasn't finding salvation on the basketball court.

Pete tried all the things the world said would make him happy: alcohol, women, and buying stuff like the latest muscle cars coming out of Detroit. But nothing gave more than fleeting satisfaction. Although he played well enough at Atlanta (the Hawks always suffered early exits from the playoffs, however), Pete found out he was dispensable when the team traded him to the New Orleans Jazz, an NBA expansion team looking for a marquee player. Sending Pete to New Orleans (the media dubbed the trade "the Louisiana Purchase") was like sending a thoroughbred to a stable filled with nags destined for the glue factory.

Pete could be excused for not remembering the names of the aging veterans, journeymen, and unproven talent who passed through New Orleans that first season. After all, twenty-two different players wore Jazz colors during the team's inaugural year. The Jazz' 23–59 record was the worst in the league.

Flashy moves seemed pointless when the team was down 20 points late in the first half, so Pete cut down on the show and started shooting more. He led the NBA in scoring with 31.1 points per game in the 1976–77 season with the Jazz, but then his body began betraying him. His physical downward slide began in January 1978, when he tore up his right knee in classic Maravich style: instead of throwing a routine outlet pass during one game, he jumped into the air and tried to whip a between-the-legs pass down the court. He landed awkwardly, badly injured his knee, and would never again play with his old joy and abandon.

Pete's knee problems were too much to overcome, and the last few seasons of Pete's NBA career were a steady descent to mediocrity. He wore the same kind of two-pound brace on his right knee that New York Jet quarterback Joe Namath did for much of his career—and suffered recurring problems in his lower back. Playing basketball with a heavy knee brace was like trying to run the court with a ball and chain. His once-quick pirouettes turned into slow-motion spinouts.

Pete's final stop in the NBA was a short-lived stint with the Boston Celtics, where he was a role player expected to drain long three-point jumpers. (The NBA had finally adopted the three-point shot at the start of the 1979–80 season.) Even though he was 10 of 15 shooting the trey during his final season, Pete couldn't defeat Father Time or his injuries. Pete walked away from the game at thirty-three years of age.

He flew home to New Orleans, where his wife, Jackie, and two-year-old son, Jaeson, were waiting for him. He made a clean break from basketball, packing his trophies and memorabilia into boxes. Anything that reminded him of the game was purged from his life—either packed away in storage or given away.

"For two years, I remained in seclusion, trying to wean myself from the effects of basketball," he wrote in *Heir to a Dream*. "At first, quitting seemed an easy proposition, but I soon discovered that leaving basketball cold turkey was the most difficult thing I had ever done. I envisioned my retirement as lazy afternoons sipping cold drinks poolside; instead I found myself wrapped in depression and self-pity, wondering what to do with all the time on my hands."

Perhaps Pete would have found happiness and peace of mind if he had become Husband of the Year to Jackie and Father of the Year to Jaeson. But it didn't work out that way. Being a loving husband and attentive dad didn't satisfy him the way he hoped it would. Plus, Jaeson was a toddler and unable to do a lot of things on his own.

Maybe putting together some great investments and increasing his net wealth would give him a sense of self-worth. But maintaining a watchful eye on the commodities and stocks he purchased caused him nothing but gut-wrenching anguish.

Maybe living longer would make life meaningful. Pete got into nutrition, thinking it would help him live to 150 years of age—and this was long before the popularity of health food stores. He tried vegetarianism for a while and filled a refrigerator with dozens of bottles of expensive vitamins and natural foods. Then he read survivalist tracts about the coming Apocalypse and toyed with the idea of building a bomb shelter where he and his family could ride out a nuclear attack.

The bomb shelter was never built.

Meanwhile, Jackie remained extremely patient with each jag that her getting-weirder-by-the-day husband chased after. His obsessive-compulsive personality pushed him into a "neat freak" stage that saw him constantly scrubbing tiles and washing dishes. Then he turned to bouts of fasting to "detox" his body of wastes and toxins. (He once fasted for twenty-five days.) Next he tried Transcendental Meditation, which was popular at the time after Maharishi Mahesh Yogi introduced TM to the Western world—via the Beatles—in the late 1960s. Pete's TM technique was a combination of teachings from Krishna, Buddha, and Shankara.

After Pete found Transcendental Meditation wanting, he turned his spiritual search toward the extraterrestrial: astrology and UFOs—unidentified flying objects. Pete even painted a message on the roof of his house to welcome any UFOs passing through the stratosphere. "Take me," the message said. Celestial exploration was another distraction from reality.

"I found nothing to hang on to that would last forever," he later wrote. "Even my greatest records would someday be broken. The trophies were collecting dust in the closet. And one day, no one would remember or even care about a floppy-socked basketball player named Pistol Pete Maravich."

But then Pete found the peace he was looking for.

One November night in 1982—two years into his hermit-like existence, which was marked by moodiness and silence—Pete couldn't fall asleep. Jackie lay dozing next to him in their bed.

The sins of Pete's youth paraded through his mind for hours. His conscience bothered him as never before. He couldn't find peace. No matter how hard he tried, he couldn't rid his mind of the guilt-inducing memories.

As early morning approached, Pete knew he had to make things right with Jesus Christ. Back when he was at LSU, he had heard the Gospel message from Bill Bright, the founder of Campus Crusade for Christ. He had seen hundreds of young people go forward, including a close friend who jumped out of his seat with tears in his eyes to give his life to Christ.

Thinking back to that event, Pete had to admit a sad truth: he had rejected Christ that day in Baton Rouge. Back then, to his way of thinking, he was going to get his championship ring in basketball, and then he'd have time for God.

But Pete never got that ring, and the acclaim he received and the cheers he heard became distant memories. As the first hints of dawn approached, he realized that his life had amounted to *nothing*.

At 5:40 a.m.—Pete remembers the time because he looked at his alarm clock—he pulled himself out of bed and got on his knees. He cried out to the Lord, saying, "I've cursed you and I've spit on you. I've mocked you and used your name in vain. I've kicked, punched, and laughed at you. Oh, God, can you forgive me? Please save me, please. I've had it with this life of mine. I've had it with all the world's answers for happiness."

An overwhelming silence filled the room, and tears flowed down the cheeks of a spiritually broken man. What Pete later remembered as an audible voice spoke to him: "Be strong. Lift thine own heart."

The words were loud and clear to him. He woke up Jackie and said, "Did you hear that? Did you hear God?"

Jackie told him that he had finally gone completely crazy, flopped her head back on the pillow, and fell back asleep.

But Pete couldn't rest. The power of God had touched him and completely changed him. From that day forward, he would give himself to serving God with all the intensity he had ever shown on a basketball court.

THE CLOCK WINDING DOWN

People who knew Pete Maravich during the last five years of his life say he couldn't go five minutes without talking about Jesus Christ.

If he was sitting in a taxi, he'd ask the cabbie if he was saved. If a total stranger was sitting next to him on a plane flight, he'd steer the friendly patter toward the topic he really wanted to talk about: Jesus Christ.

Heir to a Dream was released in October 1987 to coincide with the start of a new basketball season. The book's coda was Pete's testimony, which has been condensed for this chapter.

Having a book out gave Pete a newfound platform to share his story as well as his faith, and he gave dozens of interviews to support the launch of the book. His publisher, Thomas Nelson Publishers of Nashville, contacted Focus on the Family and asked if Dr. Dobson would be interested in interviewing Pete about his book for the daily radio program, which was heard by millions.

Focus on the Family's broadcast department forwarded the request to Dr. Dobson's office. Knowing the doctor's rabid love for basketball, I would imagine that interview request was approved faster than you could say, "Pistol Pete."

And then Dr. Dobson had another idea: invite Pete to

play basketball with him and the boys at First Church of the Nazarene. Might as well take advantage of the opportunity to play with a legend.

Audacious?

Sure. This would be like asking Willie Mays to drop by your church softball team practice or asking Arnold Palmer to show up at your men's group choose-up at the local muni.

Gary Lydic, the Focus HR director who organized the early morning games, picks up the story from here:

> I'll never forget when Dr. Dobson called me on the morning of January 4, 1988. I was in my office at Focus on the Family. He said, "Gary, you are not going to believe this. Pistol Pete Maravich is coming in tomorrow to do a broadcast, but he has also agreed to play basketball with us. I want you to get the guys together. He'll have his friend Frank Schroeder with him. Frank is the producer of the new film *Pistol*."
>
> Dr. Dobson asked me to pick up Pete and Frank at the San Dimas Inn and drive them to the First Church of the Nazarene in Pasadena—about a forty-five-minute drive in morning rush hour traffic. "Be sure to pick them up early enough so we can get started right on time," he said.
>
> "No problem, Doctor." As soon as I hung up the phone, I started calling the guys. The next day was a Tuesday, and we normally played on Mondays, Wednesdays, and Fridays. Did you think I had any trouble getting together a Tuesday game? No way! I got nothing but yeses, and they were thrilled to learn

that they were going to play basketball with Pete Maravich.

For the rest of the day, I stayed in my office and shuffled papers. I got nothing done. I kept thinking, *I get to play with Pistol Pete Maravich tomorrow! I get to pick him up!*

Back in those days, you didn't get to see the great players play like you do today. Cable TV was in its infancy, so there weren't zillions of NBA games available on ESPN or TNT. I may have seen Pete play once or twice on TV, but I certainly knew all about him from reading the newspaper and magazine stories about him.

When I got home that night, I couldn't stop talking about Pete Maravich with my bride, Debbie, and our two young sons, Trevor and Brent. I tried my best to explain what a big deal it was for me to play basketball with the famous Pistol Pete.

When I went to bed, I couldn't sleep. At two or two-thirty in the morning, I got up, grabbed my Bible, and went out to the living room. For the next few hours, I spent time with the Lord, reading and praying. I had this feeling inside me that this was going to be an incredible day.

I can't tell you how I excited I was—like a kid on Christmas morning. I kept praying that this would be a wonderful opportunity, not only for those of us who'd get a chance to play with Pete but also for Pete's chance to do the broadcast with Dr. Dobson and reach millions with his amazing testimony.

I went back to bed, but I didn't sleep a wink. I got up shortly after 5:00 a.m. to get ready for the drive to the San Dimas Inn. I was scheduled to pick up Pete and Frank at 5:30 a.m. It was pitch dark on that chilly January morning.

I pulled up to the San Dimas Inn and walked into the lobby, where I used the house phone to call Pete's room. When Pete picked up, my heart skipped a beat. "This is Gary," I said. "I'm here to pick you up."

"I'll be right down," he said. I stood in the lobby, about to meet one the best players who ever played basketball, and my knees were shaking. I had to sit down because I was so excited.

When Pete walked into the lobby, followed by Frank, he thrust out his hand. "This must be the man," he said. Introductions were made, and then we headed out to my car. Almost immediately, Pete started talking about Jesus Christ.

As we merged onto Interstate 210 into Pasadena, Pete continued talking about what Christ had been doing in his life. Even at that early time of the morning, the rush hour traffic was horrible. As we slowed into bumper-to-bumper congestion, Pete continued to describe the adventure that God had sent him on. It became apparent to me that this guy was sold out to Christ.

The longer we were stuck in traffic, though, the more I worried that we were going to be late. I decided we'd be better getting off the 210 and onto surface streets, which wouldn't be so choked with cars.

I was starting to change lanes when a car roared past and nearly clipped us. I pulled back into my lane and shot up a quick prayer: *Lord, not now, not with Pistol Pete in the car . . . any other time, but not now.*

Then, for just a moment, a thought flashed through my mind: *Maybe, just maybe, you're not supposed to be there today.* But that thought left me just as quickly as it came. I managed to get us off the freeway and onto Foothill Boulevard, but we were still twenty minutes late when we pulled into the parking lot of the First Church of the Nazarene.

When we walked inside the gym, I could see that Dr. Dobson and the guys were already playing a half-court game.

Pete, Frank, and I took the free basket on the other end of the gym and started warming up. Pete talked to me about his dad's death from cancer the previous spring. He said he took his father all over the world in private planes, trying to find a cure for him. "Gary, sometimes I took him off the plane and wasn't sure if he was still breathing or not," he said.

Pete said his dad had accepted Jesus Christ as his personal Savior before his death, and he talked about how much that meant to him. (I later learned that Pete whispered, "I'll see you soon" to his father after he took his final breath. He also told an interviewer in 1974, when talking about how his pro basketball career wasn't turning out the way he dreamt it, "I don't want to play ten years in the NBA and then die of a heart attack when I'm forty.")

I was quite moved by Pete's stories of how he cared for his father right up until the end. I looked at him, and with great emotion I said, "Pete, my dad lies in a hospital in Dayton, Ohio, and he has bone cancer."

Pete came alongside me and put an arm around my shoulders. "Gary, I've been there, and I want to walk through this with you."

I was thanking Pete when I heard Dr. Dobson's voice saying, "Come on over, guys."

We headed over to the main court, where I introduced Pete and Frank to Dr. Dobson and the rest of the guys.

Dr. Dobson was in a great mood. "Why don't you go ahead and pick the teams, Gary," he said.

Well, I've never been a very bright guy, but I decided that Pistol Pete should be on Dr. Dobson's team, and then I made sure I was part of that five-man team as well. I put our ringer, 7-foot, 2-inch Ralph Drollinger, on the other team to make things even.

Ralph had played for John Wooden at UCLA. Following graduation, he chose to play with Athletes in Action, an amateur team that toured the world playing basketball and preaching the Gospel at halftime of their games. After three seasons with Athletes in Action, Ralph played one season with the Dallas Mavericks before retiring with a lingering knee injury.

We started playing our half-court game, and

234 PLAYING WITH PURPOSE

what unfolded was just wonderful. Whenever one of us passed the ball to Pete, we stood around and watched him effortlessly dribble through his legs and make one beautiful shot after another. He took it easy, playing probably at one-third of his normal speed. He didn't have to play very hard because his competition was a bunch of out-of-shape guys in their thirties and forties huffing and puffing to keep up.

But we were all having fun, laughing, and horsing around. We played three games to ten baskets. I don't think I need to tell you who won those three games, but I happened to be on the winning team with you-know-who. Well, after the third game, we took a short break. Some of the guys went outside to get some fresh air, and some went into the hallway to get a drink from the water fountain. Before I knew it, it was just Pete, Dr. Dobson, and myself on the court.

Pete bounced a basketball near the top of the key with Dr. Dobson while taking a few shots at the basket. I stood underneath to receive the ball as it swished through the net and pump the ball back to Pete for the next shot.

Dr. Dobson asked him when he had played basketball last. Pete said he hadn't played basketball in over a year, except for an appearance at the NBA Legends game during the All-Star break the previous spring.

"Pete, how could you ever give this game up?" Dr. Dobson asked. "You love it so much, and it's so much a part of your life."

Pete replied, "You know, I didn't really realize until today how much I miss this game. I am really enjoying this, being out here with you guys."

He flexed his legs and flung another shot toward the rim. "Two weeks ago I couldn't lift my right arm up past my shoulder because I had neuritis in my right arm, and it was very, very painful."

"How do you feel today?" Dr. Dobson asked.

"I have never felt better," Pete responded. He flipped another shot toward the rim. I gathered the rebound and was starting a two-handed chest pass back to Pete when—boom . . . he fell backward like a statue, his head hitting the floor with a sickening thud.

Surely my eyes were betraying me. Dr. Dobson took a step toward him, and I did as well. Pete had a great sense of humor, and I thought that at any moment he would jump to his feet with a "gotcha" grin on his face.

But when I got to him, I saw his eyes rolling back and color draining from his face. I immediately knew he was in big trouble. Right away, Dr. Dobson lowered himself to Pete's side and started CPR chest compressions.

I ran to the doors. "Guys! Get in here! Something happened to Pete!"

Their faces were masked with concern, and I ran to the closest church office to call 911. There were no cell phones in 1988.

After I reached 911, I went to the parking lot and waited for the paramedics to arrive. The minutes ticked by like hours. It seemed like it took forever for the ambulance to arrive, but when paramedics finally arrived on the scene, I rushed them into the gym.

Dr. Dobson was still working on Pete. He pulled back as the paramedics placed defibrillation paddles on Pete's chest to restart his heart.

Dr. Dobson, the other players, and I formed a circle and began begging the Lord out loud in prayer. We were crying out, "No, not now, Lord! He just has accepted You, and all he cares about is sharing the love of Christ with everyone!"

In just an hour or two with Pete, I could see that he wanted to spend the rest of his life talking about Jesus Christ. He wanted to share with as many as he could what God had done for him—how he had tried everything that the world had to offer but was left with a huge void in his heart. When Pete found Christ, there was a total, 180-degree transformation of his life.

"Please Lord, don't take him now," we prayed out loud. "He is sharing You with everyone. He has such a strong testimony of what You have done for him."

Meanwhile, the paramedics continued to work on him, but his body was still and unresponsive. He was dead and had been since he hit the floor. The decision was made to put him on a stretcher and take him to St. Luke Hospital in Pasadena.

I remember helping the paramedics lift and place

Pete's body onto the stretcher as one of them continued to perform chest compressions. We watched as his body was loaded into the back of the ambulance. Dr. Dobson, Ralph Drollinger, and I hopped into Dr. Dobson's car to follow.

We pulled onto Sierra Madre Boulevard, but there were no sirens or red flashing lights. And the ambulance wasn't going very fast, either.

Tears poured down my face. The reality slammed into me like a crushing wave. Pete Maravich, one of the greatest basketball players ever, wasn't alive anymore.

When we got to the emergency room, the three of us sat down in the waiting room. We weren't there very long when a doctor came out and said: "Guys, I'm sorry, but Pete has died."

Hearing that statement from a medical authority, though expected, still hit me hard. The doctor invited us into the room where Pete's body lay. Never before and never since have I ever seen a more peaceful face in death. Dr. Dobson, Ralph, and I held hands around Pete's body and thanked the Lord for his life. We all knew he had gone home to be with Jesus.

But we also knew that a very difficult phone call had to be made to Pete's precious wife, Jackie Maravich, and their two little boys. Dr. Dobson left to go make that phone call. When he returned, he said, "Gary, when we get back to Focus on the Family, I want you to handle all the phone calls and all the media that is going to come in the rest of the day."

Dr. Dobson and I both knew the most important

thing to Pete was not the acclaim or scoring records, or even his notoriety, but his relationship with Jesus Christ. When I got back to the office, the phone *did* start ringing off the hook. I could not believe how quickly news of Pete's death spread. I received calls from all over the country—New York, Chicago, Atlanta, Dallas, and San Francisco—as well as calls from all around the world, including Germany, Guatemala, and Spain. The reporters and producers calling in all wanted to hear the story of what happened that morning.

By and large, the stories about Pete's death that day included a description of how he was a changed man the last five years after becoming a "born-again Christian," as the media described it. In the aftermath of Pete's passing, this was gratifying to see.

Dr. Dobson was asked to go to Baton Rouge to speak at Pete's memorial service. I was grateful that he asked me to join him. I remember reading Pete's book, *Heir to a Dream*, on the plane flight to Louisiana and meeting many of the same people that Pete wrote about in the book. These sports figures all wanted to hear about Pete's last moments on earth, and I recounted the story as I have told it here. At the memorial service, Dr. Dobson said, "Basketball at one time was his greatest love. But his greatest passion was the love of the Lord he served."

A few days after we returned to Southern California, the autopsy results came back, and they were shocking. Pete had died of a congenital heart malformation he never knew he had. In layman's terms, he was born without one of the two artery systems that supply the heart with blood. The news stunned cardiologists and other heart experts. They said most people with this condition don't live past the age of twenty—especially those who sprint up and down a basketball court for much of their lives.

In other words, Pete's heart was a ticking time bomb, and he never should have lived beyond his sophomore year at LSU.

Two weeks after Pete's death, Dr. Dobson and I met in his office. We asked each other, *Why was Pete with us when this happened?* There had to be a reason for it. And since there was a reason, what did God want us to do?

During those two weeks, I learned that Pistol Pete had his own summer basketball camps in St. Augustine, Florida. I said to Dr. Dobson: "You know, we both have been praying about what God wants us to do. We both know how Pete shared the fundamentals of the game as well as his love for Christ at his camps. What if we did a basketball camp in memory of Pistol Pete? We could share about his life and the importance of the relationship he had with the King of kings and Lord of lords. I think a basketball camp would be the most important thing that we could possibly do in his memory."

Dr. Dobson said, "Okay, run with it." So that summer at nearby Claremont-McKenna College, we held our first basketball camp in memory of Pete

Maravich. But we had a stipulation for those who wanted to come: they had to be from a single-parent family or the inner city.

That was the start of eight years of basketball camps, and what a great run we had. We traveled all over the country putting on these summer basketball camps at various colleges and universities, and we even did girls camps.

On the morning of his last hour on earth, Pete Maravich was wearing a T-shirt that read, LOOKING UNTO JESUS.

Those words come from Hebrews 12:2, which in the King James Version starts like this:

> *Looking unto Jesus the author and finisher of our faith; who for the joy that was set before him endured the cross, despising the shame, and is set down at the right hand of the throne of God.*

What a bold witness for Christ, Pete Maravich! We will never know why the Lord took Pete so suddenly and prematurely, but that is part of the sovereignty of God.

But what happened that morning at Parker Gym changed my life, and I know Pete's life and death continues to impact people nearly twenty-five years later.

A PLOT TWIST THAT HOLLYWOOD COULDN'T SCRIPT

Wasn't that quite a story from Gary Lydic?

But the narrative doesn't quite end there.

In August 1990, Dr. Dobson was playing one of his usual early morning basketball games at the First Church of the Nazarene, on the same floor where Pete Maravich had died two-and-a-half years earlier.

Dr. Dobson did not bring his best game to the gym that morning, however. In basketball lingo, he shot bricks at the glass backboard and let players drive by him like his feet were nailed to the polished hardwood floor. After blowing an easy lay-in, a sharp pain hit Dr. Dobson in the center of his chest.

As he caught his breath, he immediately knew something was not right. When his chest pains failed to diminish, he picked up his car keys and waved good-bye. "Sorry, guys, gotta go," he said as he strolled out.

It wasn't like him to quit playing basketball before 8:00 a.m. One of the players ran after Dr. Dobson, asking him if he was feeling all right. "I think I'm okay," he said, but something told Dr. Dobson that he wasn't 100 percent.

Instead of going home to shower, Dr. Dobson drove himself to the same hospital, St. Luke's of Pasadena, where paramedics had taken Pete Maravich's body. Dr. Dobson parked the car and gathered his thoughts. To march into an emergency room and announce that he was suffering chest pains would blow a huge hole in his hyper-busy schedule: meetings with the executive staff, broadcast tapings, and responding to the dozens of phone messages his personal assistants had fielded.

Dr. Dobson sat in his car for nearly thirty minutes, weighing the consequences of stepping through the emergency room doors. "What do you want me to do, Lord?" he prayed. "I'm fifty-four years old, and I'm having chest pains."

It's a good thing Dr. Dobson admitted himself at St. Luke's that morning because tests revealed that he had suffered a mild to moderate heart attack. Apparently, one of the five coronary arteries supplying his heart with blood had become blocked. Thanks to quick intervention, Dr. Dobson received the medical care he needed to stay alive.

Even though that was the last time Dr. Dobson would ever play competitive basketball, he survived a heart attack that allowed him to continue writing books, recording new broadcasts, speaking out on the issues important to families, and directing a worldwide ministry to millions of parents and children for many more years.

You have to wonder if Dr. Dobson would have ignored those chest pains if Pete Maravich hadn't died in his arms.

ABOUT THE AUTHOR

Mike Yorkey is the author, co-author, or collaborator of more than seventy-five books, including *Playing with Purpose: Inside the Lives of the NFL's Top New Quarterbacks—Sam Bradford, Colt McCoy, and Tim Tebow* and the authorized biography of Colt McCoy, *Growing Up Colt: A Father, a Son, a Life in Football*.

He has worked with a variety of athletes from different sports to help them share their stories as well as their insights, and he is the co-author of the popular Every Man's Battle series, which has two million copies in print. He is also a novelist, having co-authored *The Swiss Courier* and *Chasing Mona Lisa* (to be released in January 2012) with Tricia Goyer.

Mike Yorkey lives in the San Diego area with Nicole, his wife of thirty-two years. The Yorkeys are the parents of two adult children. His website is www.mikeyorkey.com.

SOURCE MATERIAL

Introduction: It's Not an Easy Gig, Playing in the NBA

"The NBA Player Who Never Scored" by Rick Reilly, *Sports Illustrated*, December 9, 1999, and available at http:// sportsillustrated.cnn.com/inside_game/magazine/life_of_reilly/ news/1999/12/07/life_of_reilly/

"When *Sports Illustrated* followed up with A.C. in the summer of 2008 . . ." by Adam Duerson, *Sports Illustrated*, July 14, 2008, and available at http://sportsillustrated.cnn.com/vault/article/ magazine/MAG1141820/index.htm?eref=sisf&eref=sisf

"Watching Bobby Jones on the basketball court is like watching an honest man in a liars' poker game . . . " and "He's a player who's totally selfless, who runs like a deer. . . ," both from a Bobby Jones entry on Wikipedia, available at http://en.wikipedia .org/wiki/Bobby_Jones_(basketball,_born_1951)

"Bobby didn't see what all the fuss was about . . ." from "Bobby Jones: The Gentleman of the NBA," a feature on the NBA.com website and found at http://www.nba.com/sixers/features/bobby_ jones_090506.html

1. Dr. James Naismith: Inventing with Purpose

"One time while at rugby practice . . . ," anecdote from *Big Game, Small World* by Alexander Wolff, Warner Books, New York, 2002, page 12.

"His belief was reinforced when a man from Yale University . . ." from *James Naismith: The Man Who Invented Basketball*, by Bob Rains, Hellen Carpenter Books, page 25.

"Naismith, I want you to see what you can do with those students . . . " from "Springfield College: The Birthplace of Basketball," found on the Springfield College website at http://www.springfieldcollege.edu/home.nsf/The-Birthplace-of -Basketball

4. Chris Kaman: Getting Off the Meds

"He can use both hands, and he can run the floor . . ." from "Central Michigan vs. Duke," *USA Today*, March 22, 2003, and available at http://www.usatoday.com/sports/scores103/103081/2 0030322NCAABDUKE------0nr.htm

5. Jeremy Lin: A Story Hollywood Would Have Trouble Believing

"Jeremy has a better skill set than anyone I've seen at his age . . . ," "Harvard's Hoops Star Is Asian. Why's That a Problem?" by Sean Gregory, *Time* magazine, December 31, 2009, and available at http://www.time.com/time/nation/ article/0,8599,1951044,00.html

"He knew exactly what needed to be done at every point in the basketball game . . . ," "An All-Around Talent, Obscured by His Pedigree" by Chuck Culpepper, *New York Times*, September 14, 2010, and available at http://www.nytimes.com/2010/09/15/ sports/basketball/15nba.html

"Jeremy Lin is probably one of the best players in the country you don't know about . . ." from "What They're Saying about Harvard Basketball and Jeremy," Harvard sports website, December 11, 2009, and available at http://www.gocrimson.com/sports/ mbkb/2009-10/releases/091210_MBB_Quotes

"This fascinating interview between Lacob and *San Jose Mercury News* columnist Tim Kawakami . . ." from "Lacob Interview, Part 3: On Jeremy Lin, Ellison, Larry Riley, Bold Moves, and Poker" conducted by Tim Kawakami on the Talking Points website, August 17, 2010, and available at http://blogs.mercurynews.com/ kawakami/2010/08/17/lacob-interview-part-3-on-jeremy-lin -ellison-larry-riley-bold-moves-and-poker/

6. Luke Ridnour: Heir to Pistol Pete

"Really, when I started reading the Word with my chaplain, everything changed . . ." from "Super Sonic: Seattle's Luke Ridnour Talks Small Towns and Big Faith" by Jill Ewert, *Sharing the Victory* magazine, a publication of Fellowship of Christian Athletes, and available at http://www.sharingthevictory.com/vsItemDisplay.lsp?method=display&objectid=F10AF9D8-5E91-416A-959F5BAC3AA6B942

"Coach Kent summed up his point guard's contribution this way . . ." from "Cool Hand Luke" by Jeanne Halsey, *Sports Spectrum* magazine, and available at http://faithsite.com/content.asp?SID=808&CID=59253

"My mom wouldn't be too happy about it . . ." from "The Inside Track," the *Los Angeles Times*, December 17, 2002, and available at http://articles.latimes.com/2002/dec/17/sports/sp-quotebook17

"You must have made a big impression on him, then . . ." from "Super Couple: Kate Ridnour Q&A" by Jill Ewert, *Sharing the Victory* magazine, a publication of Fellowship of Christian Athletes, and available at http://www.sharingthevictory.com/vsItemDisplay.lsp&objectID=E22C67AB-BE6F-4326-86C9D58F7DC1BC2B&method=display

7. They're Playing with Purpose, Too

"It turns out that Dr. Orsino is a blogger . . ." from a blog called "End of Me" by Guy Stanton, April 21, 2008, and available at http://stantonmarcfreyendofme.blogspot.com/2008/04/stephen-curry-i-can-do-all-things.html

"I have like a deal for my pastor . . ." from "Brazil's Nene Vows to Retire by 2016 Olympics to Focus on Religion" by Chris Tomassen, *AOL News*, October 4, 2009, and available at http://www.aolnews.com/2009/10/04/brazils-nene-vows-to-retire-by-2016-olympics-to-focus-on-religi/

"It was scary, but I believe in God . . ." from "Nene 'a Survivor' after Cancerous Testicle Removed" by Benjamin Hockman, *Denver Post*, March 8, 2008, and available at http://webcache .googleusercontent.com/search?q=cache:asPckLRh0aAJ:www .denverpost.com/ci_8498637%3Fsource%3Dbb+nene+a+survivo r+after+cancerous+testicle+removed&cd=2&hl=en&ct=clnk&gl =us&source=www.google.com

"It's a good play for our defense . . . " from "Feisty Nick Collison Takes Charge" by Mike Baldwin, *The Oklahoman* newspaper, March 9, 2010, and available at http://newsok.com/fiesty-nick -collison-takes-charge/article/3444923

"In short, Kevin Durant is endorsement gold right now . . ." from "Kevin Durant is D'Man: An Endorsement Diamond in the Midwestern Rough" by Patrick Rishe, *Forbes* magazine, May 20, 2011, and available at http://blogs.forbes.com/ sportsmoney/2011/05/20/kevin-durant-is-dman-an -endorsement-diamond-in-the-midwestern-rough/

"It's tough, man. I can't lie about that . . ." from "NBA All-Star Kevin Durant on Faith, Family, and Fame" by Chad Bonham of *Inspiring Athletes*, and available at http://blog.beliefnet.com/ inspiringathletes/2011/05/nba-all-star-kevin-durant-on-faith -family-and-fame.html

"I'm keeping strong at it, just trying to make my walk with faith a little better . . ." from "Thunder's Kevin Durant Commits to Daily Bible Reading'" by Darnell Mayberry, *The Oklahoman* newspaper, April 21, 2011, and available at http://newsok.com/thunders -kevin-durant-commits-to-daily-bible-reading/article/3560862

"I've got Jesus in my heart . . . " from "Bill Sorrell: Faith Sustains Young Griz Players" by Bill Sorrell, published on the FaithinMemphis website on April 8, 2011, and available at http:// faithinmemphis.com/2011/04/08/bill-sorrell-faith-sustains -young-griz-players/

"It helps me in every aspect of my life . . ." from "NBA Rookie in the Habit of Thanking God" by Lee Warren, *Christian Post*, May 11, 2011, and available at http://www.christianpost.com/news/nba-rookie-in-the-habit-of-thanking-god-50190/

"I'm lucky to get a second chance . . ." from "Heart Conditions Ends Notre Dame Player's Career," *Los Angeles Times*, September 29, 1990, and available at http://articles.latimes.com/1990-09-29/sports/sp-1229_1_notre-dame

"To this day, the doctors can't understand what happened . . . " from "A Perfect Character for the Blazers" by Brian Meehan, The Oregonian newspaper, August 21, 2005, and available at http://www.4hcm.org/forums/archive/index.php/t-10311.html

"We came up with a tool that will help people take certain verses and chew on those verses for a week . . ." from "New Orleans Hornets Coach Monty Williams Lifted by Faith" by Jimmy Smith, the *New Orleans Times-Picayune* newspaper, December 25, 2010, and available at http://blog.nola.com/hornets_impact/print.html?entry=/2010/12/new_orleans_hornets_coach_mont_22.html

Overtime: Pistol Pete Maravich, the Prodigal Who Played with Purpose

"His canvas was the basketball floor, and his brush was his basketball . . . " from "Sixty Cool Pistol Pete Facts," compiled by John Hareas, Andrew Pearson, and Chad Sanders for the nba.com website and available at http://www.nba.com/features/sixty_pistol_pete_facts_070622.html

"Whenever I went to the movies I'd take my ball with me . . ." from "I Want to Put on a Show" by Pete Maravich with Curry Kirkpatrick, *Sports Illustrated*, December 1, 1969, and available at http://sportsillustrated.cnn.com/vault/article/magazine/MAG1083101/index.htm

"A former teammate, "Sweet Lou" Hudson, summed it up this way . . ." from "No One Can Cap the Pistol" by Curry Kirkpatrick, *Sports Illustrated*, December 4, 1978, and available at http://sportsillustrated.cnn.com/vault/article/magazine/MAG1094399/index.htm

"Then he tore up one knee in classic Maravich style . ." from "NBA Encyclopedia: Pistol Pete Maravich," found on the nba.com website and available at http://www.nba.com/history/players/maravich_bio.html

"For two years, I remained in seclusion . . ." from *Heir to a Dream* by Pete Maravich and Darrel Campbell, Thomas Nelson Publishers, 1987, page 187.

"I don't want to play ten years [in the NBA] and then die of a heart attack when I'm forty. . . " from "Maravich's Creative Artistry Dazzled" by Bob Carter, a SportsCenter Biography on the espn.com website and available at http://espn.go.com/classic/biography/s/Maravich_Pete.html

"Even my greatest records would someday be broken . . ." from *Heir to a Dream*, by Pete Maravich and Darrel Campbell, Thomas Nelson Publishers, 1987, page 189.

"I've cursed you and I've spit on you . . ." from *Heir to a Dream* by Pete Maravich and Darrel Campbell, Thomas Nelson Publishers, 1987, page 190.

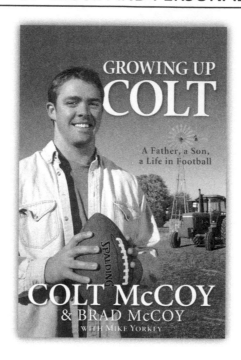